INVISIBLE BARRIERS TO INVISIBLE TRADE

Also published for the Trade Policy Research Centre by Macmillan

TOWARDS AN OPEN WORLD ECONOMY
by Frank McFadzean *et al.*

WORLD AGRICULTURE IN DISARRAY
by D. Gale Johnson

THE ESSENTIALS OF ECONOMIC INTEGRATION
by Victoria Curzon

NEGOTIATING ON NON-TARIFF DISTORTIONS
OF TRADE
by Robert Middleton

INVISIBLE BARRIERS TO
INVISIBLE TRADE

by

BRIAN GRIFFITHS

HOLMES & MEIER PUBLISHERS, INC.
IMPORT DIVISION
101 Fifth Avenue, New York, N. Y. 10003

© *Trade Policy Research Centre 1975*

First published 1975 by
THE MACMILLAN PRESS LTD
*London and Basingstoke
Associated companies in New York
Dublin Melbourne Johannesburg and Madras*

SBN 333 18533 1

Typeset by
COLD COMPOSITION LTD
Southborough, Tunbridge Wells

Printed in Great Britain by
UNWIN BROTHERS LTD
Woking and London

Trade Policy Research Centre London

The Trade Policy Research Centre in London was established in 1968 to promote independent analysis and public discussion of commercial and other international economic policy issues. It is a privately sponsored non-profit organization and is essentially an entrepreneurial centre under the auspices of which a variety of activities are conducted. As such, the Centre provides a focal point for those in business, the universities and public affairs who are interested in international economic questions.

The Centre is managed by a Council which is headed by Sir Frank McFadzean, Chairman of the "Shell" Transport

and Trading Company. The members of the Council, set out above, represent a wide range of experience and expertise.

Having general terms of reference, the Centre does not represent any consensus of opinion. Intense international competition, technological advances in industry and agriculture and new and expanding markets, together with large-scale capital flows, are having profound and continuing effects on international production and trading patterns. With the increasing integration and interdependence of the world economy there is thus a growing necessity to increase public understanding of the problems now being posed and of the kind of solutions that will be required to overcome them.

The principal function of the Centre is the sponsorship of research programmes on policy problems of national and international importance. Specialists in universities and private firms are commissioned to carry out the research and the results are published and circulated in academic, business and government circles throughout the European Community and in other countries. Meetings and seminars are also organized from time to time.

Publications are presented as professionally competent studies worthy of public consideration. The interpretations and conclusions in them are those of their authors and do not purport to represent the views of the Council and others associated with the Centre.

The Centre, which is registered in the United Kingdom as an educational trust under the Charities Act 1960, and its research programmes are financed by foundation grants, corporate donations and membership subscriptions.

Contents

Trade Policy Research Centre   v

List of Tables   xi

Biographical Note   xii

Foreword   xiii

Preface   xv

Abbreviations   xvii

1   **Nature and Importance of Trade in Invisibles**   1

   Outline of the Study   2
   Components of Invisible Trade   4
     Transport   4
     Travel   5
     Other Services   5
     Interest, Profits and Dividends   6
     Private Transfers   7
   WORLD INVISIBLE TRADE   7
   British Invisible Trade   14
   Growth of World Capital Markets   21

2   **Analysis of Barriers to Invisible Trade**   31

   Flow of Current Services   31
   Movement of Capital   33
     Direct Investment   33
     Portfolio Investment   34
   Types of Constraints   34

vii

FINANCIAL AND TRANSPORT SERVICES   35
   Restriction of Foreign Competition   35
   Government Procurement   37
   Exchange Control   38

MOVEMENT OF CAPITAL   39
   DIRECT INVESTMENT   39
   Restriction of Foreign Competition   39
   Constraints on Choice of Product Mix   40
   Constraints on Choice of Factor-Input Mix   41
   PORTFOLIO INVESTMENT   41
   Control of Interest Payments on Deposits   42
   Restraints on Foreign Borrowing and Lending   42
   Fiscal Measures   43
   Reserve Requirements   43
   Exchange Control   44

CONSTRAINTS IN PARTICULAR FIELDS   44
   SERVICES   45
   Insurance Case Study   45
      Restriction of Foreign Competition   48
      Measures for Exchange Control   52
      Government Discrimination   53
      Employment of Expatriates   56
   Banking   56
   Shipping   58
      Flag Discrimination   58
      Cabotage Laws   59
      Operating Subsidies   60
   Travel   61

   MONETARY MOVEMENTS   61
   Direct Investment   61
   Portfolio Investment   63

3   Defence of the Barriers to Invisible Trade   67

      Infant Industry Argument   70
      Domestic Ownership of Key Industries   72
      Foreign Banks and Monetary Policy   73
      Retaliation against the Constraints of Other
          Countries   75
      Need for Balanced Growth   79
      Short-term Capital Movements   79

4   Global Approach to Constraints on
    Invisible Trade   83

      Evaluation of OECD Measures   87
      Possible Forms of Action   91
        Retaliation   91
        Bilateral Agreements   92
        GATT-Style Multilateral Negotiations   93
        Codes of Conduct   95
        Unilateral Action   96
      General Code on Invisibles and Capital
          Movements   97
        Financial Services: Banking   98
        Transport: Shipping   98
        Portfolio Capital   102
      Policy for Broaching Constraints on Invisibles   103
        Rey Report and Services   104
        McFadzean Report and Earnings from
            Investments   106

    Appendix 1   113

      Illustrative List of Discriminatory Constraints
      on Invisible Earnings

        Banking   114
        Direct Investment   122

Insurance	133
Shipping	143
Travel	152

Appendix 2

155

Extracts from the OECD Code for the
Liberalization of Capital Movements

Appendix 3

159

OECD Code of Liberalization of Current Invisible
Operations

Selected Bibliography	169
Index	175

List of Tables

1   World Trade by Main Categories: 1960, 1964 and
    1968-71   8

2   Balances of Invisible Trade, Visible Trade and
    Current Account: 1971   10

3   Measures of Dependence on Invisible Trade:
    1960, 1964 and 1971   12

4   Top Ten Invisible Earners: 1970 and 1971   15

5   Invisibles in the United Kingdom's Current
    Account: 1960-73   16

6   Invisibles in the United Kingdom's Current
    Account: 1955-71   16

7   Analysis of Invisibles in the United Kingdom's
    Balance of Payments: 1962-72   18

8   External Liabilities and Claims of Banks in the
    United Kingdom in Non-Sterling Currencies:
    1963-73   22

9   Growth of Euro-Currency Markets: 1966-71   24

10 Foreign Bond Issues: 1958-68   26

11 New Issues of International Bonds in North
    America and Western Europe, 1963- mid-1971   28

Biographical Note

BRIAN GRIFFITHS, a Lecturer in Economics at the London School of Economics and Political Science since 1965, has taken a special interest in banking and writes extensively on the subject. In 1969 he was a visiting economist at the Banco de Mexico and in 1972-3 a Visiting Professor at the University of Rochester in the United States.

Mr Griffiths has also taught at the Civil Service Staff College and acted as a consultant to various financial bodies. He is the author of *Competition in Banking* (1970) and *Mexican Monetary Policy and Economic Development* (1972) and has contributed to various academic and banking journals.

Foreword

The service industries are an important earner of foreign exchange for the United Kingdom as they are for many other industrialized countries. In fact services, particularly financial and commercial ones, are likely to loom larger in the world economy as more and more countries industrialize. In due course, therefore, the conduct of international transactions in invisibles is likely to become a matter of increasing inter-governmental concern and the removal of obstacles to such commerce a prime aim of government.

In this pioneer study sponsored by the Trade Policy Research Centre a preliminary effort is made to identify such obstacles. The field of invisibles has not been subject to such a general overview before, although some work, of varying quality, has been done on specific aspects.

The study was made possible by a grant from the Nuffield Foundation and by funds made available by the British National Export Council (since replaced by the British Overseas Trade Board) through the Committee on Invisible Exports. The Centre has been extremely grateful for this support and encouragement.

As with all work sponsored by the Centre, the author of this report is entirely responsible for its analysis and conclusions; the views expressed do not necessarily represent those of others associated with the Centre, the purpose of which is to promote independent research and public discussion of international economic policy issues.

HUGH CORBET
Director
Trade Policy Research Centre

London
Spring 1975

Preface

This study for the Trade Policy Research Centre has taken considerably longer to reach fruition than was originally intended. While certain specific aspects of "invisible" transactions have received close attention, the field, taken as a whole, is still relatively neglected. Very little reliable data is available on which international comparisons might be made. Obtaining full enough information on which to proceed has therefore been a major difficulty. All that has been possible here is for a beginning to be made on opening up the subject for closer discussion and analysis.

I have been extremely grateful to the Trade Policy Research Centre for the opportunity to do the study. Thanks are due to William Clarke and Paul Stonham for introducing me to the whole complex subject and for helping me over many difficulties. I am also grateful to Harry G. Johnson, the Centre's Director of Studies, and to Max Corden for their extremely useful criticism of an earlier draft, as well as to Hugh Corbet, the Director of the Centre, from whom I received enormous help and encouragement.

Very generous help with information was also given to me by officials in organisations associated with the various branches of the service sector in the United Kingdom. A great many people employed in the fields of banking, insurance, merchanting, shipping and travel in Belgium, Britain, Canada, France, Germany, Switzerland and the United States also helped in my enquiries. I have benefited, too, from discussions with officials of the OECD, GATT and UNCTAD secretariats, with others in the Treasury and the Departments of Trade and Industry in the United Kingdom, and with still others in the Treasury and Federal Reserve System in the United States.

During much of the exercise I had the research assistance of Forest Capie. Judith Flynn and Janet Strachan put the final draft in proper editorial shape and Margaret Bacciarelli prepared the final typescript. Their patience and fortitude was much appreciated.

While acknowledging the help of those mentioned above, it has to be said they bear no responsibility for what has been written, especially for any judgments, whether implicit or explicit.

London
Spring 1975

BRIAN GRIFFITHS

Abbreviations

BEI	European Investment Bank
CENSA	Committee of European National Shipowners Association
CICA	International Conference of African, French and Malagasy States on Insurance Supervision
c.i.f.	cost, insurance and freight, prices including
EEC	European [Economic] Community
EFTA	European Free Trade Association
f.o.b.	free-on-board prices
GATT	General Agreement on Tariffs and Trade
GNP	gross national product
IATA	International Air Transport Association
IMF	International Monetary Fund
MFN	most favoured nation, referring to international treatment or to tariff levels
OECD	Organization for Economic Cooperation and Development
OEEC	Organization for European Economic Cooperation
UNCTAD	United Nations Conference on Trade and Development

CHAPTER 1

Nature and Importance of Trade in Invisibles

One of the earliest contributions to the study of non-tariff barriers to visible trade was a book entitled *The Invisible Tariff*.[1] The term "non-tariff barriers", now in common usage, refers to policies and practices which either by design or accident protect or favour domestic producers *vis-à-vis* foreign suppliers − at the expense of domestic consumers and taxpayers. Some of them are not barriers, but serve instead to encourage exports, which is why economic purists prefer the term "non-tariff distortions" or "non-tariff interventions".[2] But this is by the way. The barriers to, or constraints on, international trade in what are called "invisibles" are of a non-tariff character. The temptation to call this volume *Invisible Barriers to Invisible Trade* was thus too great.

Constraints on earnings from trade in invisibles make up an enormous subject that is still comparatively uncharted. For they are not measures conveniently listed in a manual. The issues involved cover *inter alia* the exclusion of commercial banks from certain countries, bilateral shipping agreements between governments, controls by industrial countries on the inflow of short-term capital and cartel arrangements in the field of civil aviation. The variety of measures is extremely wide. This is not surprising in view of the heterogeneity of the items included under the heading of "invisible earnings" in the standard balance-of-payments classification − as set out in the *Balance of Payments Manual* of the International Monetary Fund (IMF). And within each category of invisible trade there is a surprisingly large number of constraints on the business of foreign interests. But in discussing them, reference will be made, in this study, to British experience.

What is meant by "invisible" trade? At first sight the expression seems to be something of a paradox. How can transactions between the residents of different countries, which are real enough to the parties concerned, somehow be termed "invisible"? The paradox can be resolved by considering the different kinds of transactions that take place between countries and which, as a consequence, are recorded in the balance-of-payments accounts.

Such exchanges can be of many different kinds: the sale of an Italian car in Germany or the purchase by a resident of France of a Japanese radio; the provision of banking services by a Dutch bank to Californians; the purchase of an insurance policy by a British firm from a Canadian life assurance company; the shipping of oil from the Middle East to Belgium in a Liberian tanker; the royalties from a French film being shown in Australia; the purchase by a resident of the United Kingdom of equity shares on the New York Stock Exchange; the sale of British treasury bills to the Nigerian Government, and so on.

The movement of physical goods such as cars, radios, metals and grain between countries is termed "visible" trade. Goods which move through customs barriers can be seen and inspected. But the selling and buying of services between countries cannot be seen and inspected. The British bank which supplies banking services in New York does not have its services examined by customs authorities.

Invisible transactions, or more strictly transactions in invisibles, record the imports and exports of services between a particular country and the rest of the world: interest, profit and dividend receipts and payments connected with direct, portfolio and other foreign investment;[3] and unilateral transfer payments, for which there is no *quid pro quo,* such as gifts. The crucial distinction therefore between visible and invisible trade is that the first refers to trade in merchandise while the other refers to trade in services and flows of income earned on capital and of financial transfers.

Outline of the Study

The object of the study has been to analyse the major constraints on the invisible earnings of countries, focusing in particular on those of the United Kingdom, and to suggest measures that could lead to the liberalization of this field of international exchange. Because the subject is so vast, and because relatively little has been done to consider the problem of restrictions to invisible trade *as a whole,* this enquiry has been more in the nature of an exploratory survey of the field. In fact, because of the difficulties in obtaining reliable information, in spite of a great deal of help from various quarters, a number of categories of invisible earnings have not been explored as deeply as originally intended. The study should not be regarded therefore as a thoroughly comprehensive one. But a beginning has been made for others to develop.

None of this is to deny that much valuable work has been done in the past. But previously the approach has been either to consider restrictions on payments only in relation to the whole range of invisible earnings,[4] or to consider only certain types of restrictions which can be regarded as "non-tariff barriers" to invisible trade,[5] or to consider only one category of invisible activity.[6] Only recently have invisibles come to be recognized, at a high policy level, as an area affecting international economic relations.[7] But they have not yet reached the agenda of a general international negotiation under the auspices of either the IMF or, perhaps more appropriately, the General Agreement on Tariffs and Trade (GATT) — the instrument by which international trade has been governed since the end of the Second World War.

After describing the various items included under invisibles and dwelling on the importance of invisible trade, the second chapter attempts to list and analyse, somewhat briefly, the constraints on earnings from services and capital investments. Securing information on such constraints is far more difficult than might be imagined. There is no single source and on some constraints there is no published material at all. Because of this a survey, based on a questionnaire to governments, was conducted with partial results. This last was only to be expected with a non-official exercise supported by limited resources. But an inter-governmental inventory of constraints would yield much greater dividends. In the third chapter an attempt is made to analyse the arguments which are put forward by countries to defend the imposition of constraints on non-nationals. The fourth chapter is devoted to an examination of the work of the Organization for Economic Cooperation and Development (OECD) in the field of invisibles and proposals for policy-makers are advanced for consideration.

Components of Invisible Trade

The major components of a country's invisible trade are classified in balance-of-payments statistics as (i) government services and transfers; (ii) other services which include, *inter alia*, those connected with insurance, banking, merchanting, brokerage, royalties, films and television and postal services; (iii) interest, profits and dividends on direct, portfolio and other investments; and lastly (iv) private transfers. Apart from government services, some of the other categories cover transactions in both the public and private sector.

Government services and transfers include: military, administrative and diplomatic expenditures; economic grants made to developing countries; military grants made and received; subscriptions to various international bodies to meet their administrative expenses and contributions to international organizations to assist developing countries; and various other transfers.

Transport

A major component of invisible trade is transport and transactions under this head include port charges, passenger fares paid to overseas airlines and airport landing fees. The two main areas of transport are broken down as follows:

Shipping Transactions under the heading of shipping cover both dry cargo and tanker ships. Receipts include earnings from the country's ships (either owned by, or chartered to, the country concerned) in the carriage of exports, freight on cross trades, passenger revenue collected abroad, time charter hire from abroad and disbursements of foreign ships in the ports of the country. Payments abroad include charter hire for foreign vessels, freight and passenger payments to overseas operators and various disbursements such as canal dues, port charges, handling charges, payments for bunkers *et cetera.* Balance-of-payments statistics for shipping also record freight on imports earned by the country's ships and by ships on charter to the country's owners and passenger revenue collected in the country. If it were not for the existence of the country's merchant fleet, these freights would be earned by foreign ships, which means they are gross import savings.

Civil aviation Payments to a country's airlines by overseas residents for passenger fares, freight on cross trades, carriage of the country's exports, mail and charter hire and various expenditure in the country by foreign airlines are included under the heading of civil aviation earnings. Payments abroad include passenger and freight fares paid to overseas airlines and expenditures by the country's own airlines on such items as airport landing fees, handling charges, operating cost of overseas offices and so on.

Travel

Travel covers expenditure by residents of the country when in other countries and expenditure by residents of other countries when in the country in question.

Other Services

The transactions in services between the private residents of one country and those of another (whether private or government) which cannot be included in any other category are given here. Some of the most important to this study are briefly discussed below.

Insurance Net earnings from abroad[8] of insurers from life insurance and from fire, accident and marine insurance, including that from underwriters and brokers (such as those associated with Lloyds in Britain), but excluding income from investment in foreign securities held by insurers.

Banking Net earnings from abroad[9] of discount houses, commercial banks, merchant banks and foreign overseas banks for such services as money and credit transfer, foreign-exchange dealing and arbitrage, credit and bill business, new security issues and personal finance advice, arbitrage and underwriting and financing of overseas trade.

Merchanting   Net earnings from commodity trading and other transactions in goods not touching equity shares.

Brokerage   Net earnings from the chartering and, also, from the sales and purchases of ships and aircraft; from stock exchange dealings and other miscellaneous activities, such as those of Lloyds Register of Shipping.

Commission on exports and imports   Earnings of agents acting on behalf of foreign exporters to the country and of agents abroad acting for the country's exporters to the rest of the world.

Films, television and royalties   This item is concerned with overseas transactions with respect to the production costs, royalties, rentals and purchases of cinematograph films and television material; and, also, with the net earnings from royalties, licenses to use patents, trade marks, designs, copyrights, manufacturing rights and use of technical "know how" and mineral royalties.

Miscellaneous services   Charges for serviced supplies between related companies (for example, management expenses, commissions, branch contributions to head office expenses), agency expenses, advertising and other commercial services rendered between non-related companies, consultancy fees, construction work, fees for other professional services, expenditure by overseas students and journalists, overseas governments' diplomatic expenditure in the country concerned and a million and one other things.

Interest, Profits and Dividends

Included under the item "interest, profits and dividends" in the balance-of-payments classification are interest, profit and dividend payments either to or by residents of the country. There are three main categories which relate to the type of investment:

Direct investment income   Earnings from overseas branches of domestic companies, interest payments for loans granted to subsidiaries and dividends paid by them, and the parent companies' share of profits which have been retained by the subsidiary companies for the purpose of reinvestment. But this item excludes the earnings of oil companies.

Portfolio investment income   Remitted interest and dividends. Debits are interest and dividends on company securities and public sector stocks and issues which are held by overseas residents. And credits include dividends and interest paid to residents of the country by foreign companies and governments.

Other investment income   The most important item included under this category for the United Kingdom has been the earnings of British oil companies, which include the profits of oil companies overseas adjusted for the value of services rendered between parent companies, overseas subsidiaries and associated companies. On the debit side is the corresponding profit, interest and dividends of the subsidiaries of foreign oil companies.

Private Transfers

Transfers between private individuals related to gifts either in cash or in kind between the private residents of a country and private residents of another country.

WORLD INVISIBLE TRADE

The process of economic growth is accompanied by a progressive transfer from agriculture to industry and from industry to services. In the economies of the developed countries, services already constitute a substantial part of the national product, employing a large proportion of the labour force. In the United States and Canada, services contribute about 60 per cent of the gross national product (GNP), and about the same percentage of the labour force. In West Germany, France, Japan and the United Kingdom the share of services in the GNP ranges from 40 to 60 per cent and in the labour force from 40 to 50 per cent. This trend can be expected to continue.

Invisible Barriers to Invisible Trade

Table 1 WORLD TRADE BY MAIN

	1960		1964	
	Receipts	Payments	Receipts	Payments
VISIBLE TRADE	102,800	101,000	143,600	139,000
1. Merchandise	101,700	100,800	142,300	138,600
2. Non-monetary Gold	1,100	200	1,300	400
INVISIBLE TRADE	31,400	30,500	45,800	44,500
3, 4. Transport	9,900	10,600	13,800	14,400
5. Foreign Travel	6,100	5,700	9,700	8,900
6. Investment Income	8,800	8,200	12,600	12,000
8. Other Services	6,600	6,000	9,700	9,200
GOVERNMENT AND TRANSFERS	8,500	11,000	11,200	14,200
7. Government n.i.e.	4,400	5,400	5,400	6,400
9. Private Donations	2,300	2,100	3,800	3,500
10. Official Donations	1,800	3,500	2,000	4,300
TOTAL TRADE (Items 1–10)	142,700	142,500	200,600	197,700
Total Trade exc. items 7, 9 and 10	134,100	131,500	189,400	183,500
Invisible Trade/Total Trade exc. items 7, 9 and 10	23.4%	23.2%	24.2%	24.3%
Government and Transfers/ Total Trade (Items 1–10)	6.0%	7.7%	5.6%	7.2%
Transport/Invisible Trade	31.4%	34.6%	30.1%	32.4%
Foreign Travel/Invisible Trade	19.5%	18.6%	21.2%	20.0%
Investment Income/Invisible Trade	28.0%	27.0%	27.5%	27.0%
Other Services/Invisible Trade	21.1%	19.8%	21.2%	20.7%

Source: World Invisible Trade (London: Committee on Invisible Exports, 1974), based

Many activities in the services sector do not give rise to international transactions. But there are important areas in which international exchanges have risen steeply; indeed, they have been rising as fast as, if not faster than, international exchanges in merchandise. Invisibles now account for about one-quarter to one third of all current international payments. The importance of services in external transactions varies considerably from country to country. Much depends on structural factors. But services, like industrial production, are experiencing a considerable degree of internationalization.

CATEGORIES: 1960, 1964 and 1968-71 ($m)

1968		1969		1970		1971	
Receipts	Payments	Receipts	Payments	Receipts	Payments	Receipts	Payments
190,400	187,100	239,700	241,000	276,300	282,100	308,400	311,810
189,000	186,500	238,000	240,100	274,700	281,400	306,900	310,800
1,400	600	1,700	900	1,600	700	1,500	1,010
67,600	66,500	78,100	79,000	92,770	93,380	106,305	104,555
19,800	20,500	21,500	22,600	25,900	28,325	29,500	31,650
14,300	13,100	17,000	15,400	20,700	18,285	24,100	21,075
18,700	19,100	22,700	24,000	26,570	28,200	29,510	30,970
14,800	13,800	16,900	17,000	19,600	18,570	23,195	20,860
15,700	21,600	22,100	23,800	24,200	26,400	28,695	30,535
7,800	9,500	8,500	10,100	8,800	10,700	10,280	11,785
5,400	5,400	9,600	7,100	10,600	8,000	11,990	8,980
2,500	6,700	4,000	6.600	4,800	7,700	6,425	9,770
273,700	275,200	339,900	343,800	393,270	401,880	443,400	446,900
258,000	253,600	317,800	320,000	369,070	375,480	414,705	416,365
26.2%	26.2%	24.6%	24.7%	25.2%	24.9%	25.6%	25.1%
5.5%	7.8%	6.5%	6.9%	6.1%	6.6%	6.5%	6.8%
29.3%	30.8%	27.5%	28.6%	27.9%	30.3%	27.8%	30.3%
21.2%	19.7%	21.8%	19.5%	22.3%	19.6%	22.7%	20.2%
27.7%	28.7%	29.1%	30.4%	28.7%	30.2%	27.8%	29.6%
21.9%	20.8%	21.6%	21.5%	21.1%	19.9%	21.8%	20.0%

on material collected by the International Monetary Fund.

The quadrupling of the price of oil at the end of 1973 gave a further impetus to international transactions in the service sector — although it should not be exaggerated. For in order to diversify their economies, putting vastly increased revenues from oil into industrial and infra-structure developments, the oil-producing countries have been expected to require foreign services, particularly managerial, engineering and educational services. The import-absorption capacity of the oil-producing countries, even the dessert economies, will grow as their increased incomes enables them to purchase organizational ability from abroad.

Invisible Barriers to Invisible Trade

Table 2

BALANCES OF INVISIBLE TRADE, VISIBLE TRADE
AND CURRENT ACCOUNT: 1971

($m)

Country	Invisible balance	Visible balance	Transfers and govt. spending	Current balance
United States	8,750	−2,693	−6,289	−232
United Kingdom	2,741	763	−1,008	2,496
European Community				
France	881	1,106	−1,588	449
Italy	1,427	114	23	1,564
West Germany	−4,801	6,369	−1,401	167
Netherlands	558	−717	−103	−262
Belgium-Luxembourg[a]	96	846	−94	848
Other Western Europe				
Norway	923	−1,436	8	−505
Switzerland[a]	1,823	−1,366	−377	80
Sweden[a]	−34	396	−176	186
Austria	736	—884	57	−91
Denmark[a, b]	266	−668	−44	−446
Portugal[a, c]	322	−810	670	182
Finland[a]	117	−456	−1	−340
Spain	1,686	−1,599	769	856
Yugoslavia[a]	938	−1,435	140	−357
Greece[a]	481	−1,320	464	−375
Ireland[a, d]	212	−524	107	−205
Other developed countries				
Japan	−2,325	7,787	335	5,797
Canada	−2,454	2,592	255	393
Australia	−1,277	597	−204	−884
South Africa	−811	−604	49	-1,366
Lesser developed countries				
Mexico[a]	38	−903	59	−806
Israel	25	−645	247	−373
Argentina[a]	−292	−129	31	−390
TOTAL 'TOP 25'	10,026	4,381	−8,021	6,386

Source: *World Invisible Trade* (London: Committee on Invisible Exports, 1974), based on material collected by the International Monetary Fund.

Note: No sign indicates a credit whereas the minus sign indicates a debit.

a Some or all merchandise imports valued c.i.f.

b Merchandise insurance normally included in transport figures not available separately and partly included in visible trade and partly in other services.

c Figures for metropolitan Portugal and overseas territories with the rest of the world; the credit entries on freight are believed not to include Portuguese freight earnings on imports by the overseas territories from foreign countries even though these imports are shown c.i.f.

d Insurance on merchandise (other than that included in the c.i.f. value of imports) is appropriate to transport, but figures are not available.

It was mainly providers of managerial and technological "know how", as well as providers of financial services, that pressed in the United States for the inclusion of services in the Administration's negotiating authority for the Tokyo Round of GATT negotiations, as sought from Congress in the Trade Act of 1974. In the legislation it is specifically stated that the term "international trade" includes trade in both goods and services. Whether the Tokyo Round negotiations deal with services remains to be seen. But the subject is likely to be on the agenda of future GATT deliberations.

The importance of invisible trade to the world as a whole is shown in Table 1.[10] If invisible trade is measured excluding both the value of government services which are traded between countries and the value of inter-governmental grants and loans, then the ratio of the total value of invisible trade, either on a payments or on a receipts basis,[11] was just over 26 per cent in 1968, but declined again in the subsequent two years. Between 1960 and 1968 world invisible trade grew at a more rapid pace than visible trade. The ratio of invisible trade to visible trade rose over this period from approximately 23 to 26 per cent.

The breakdown of world invisible trade between transport, foreign travel, investment income and other services is also shown in Table 1. Although transport as a proportion of total invisible trade fell slightly over the 1960s, and foreign travel as a proportion of world invisible trade rose over the same period, the interesting feature of these figures is the stability of the ratios of individual categories of invisible trade to the total of invisible trade through the decade. Transport accounts for approximately 30 per cent of world invisible trade; foreign travel, for approximately 20 per cent; investment income, for just under 30 per cent; and other services, for just over 20 per cent.

While there is a tendency for developed countries to have a surplus on their invisible accounts, and other countries to have a deficit, the pattern is by no means uniform. In Table 2 the visible and invisible balances of the leading 25 countries in invisible trade are shown for the year 1970. The two most important countries in invisible trade are the United States and the United Kingdom which both have

Invisible Barriers to Invisible Trade

Table 3 MEASURES OF DEPENDENCE ON

Country	Invisible Receipts as % of Total Receipts		
	1960	1964	1971
United States	29.0	30.6	34.1
United Kingdom	33.3	33.4	35.8
European Community			
France a	–	–	26.1
Italy	30.6	30.5	30.0
West Germany	13.0	13.9	15.4
Netherlands	23.7	25.6	25.9
Belgium-Luxembourg	19.6	17.9	22.2
Other Western Europe			
Norway	51.5	48.9	49.7
Switzerland	30.2	31.2	33.6
Sweden	23.1	19.9	19.2
Austria	21.7	31.3	35.5
Denmark	23.7	23.2	26.1
Portugal	17.8	27.2	37.3
Finland	14.7	17.4	21.8
Spain	29.8	45.0	48.7
Yugoslavia b	16.2	24.5	46.0
Greece	29.2	35.3	53.5
Ireland	34.9	32.3	27.6
Other developed countries			
Japan	10.5	12.2	14.8
Canada	14.9	15.2	15.3
Australia	12.2	15.9	17.8
South Africa	10.0	9.9	20.4
Lesser developed countries			
Mexico b	41.6	40.6	53.4
Israel	18.3	26.0	45.3
Argentina c	14.0	9.3	17.1
TOTAL 'TOP 25'	24.3	25.2	26.9
REST OF WORLD	13.7	14.6	12.8
WORLD	22.0	22.8	24.0

Source: World Invisible Trade (London: Committee on Invisible Exports, 1974), based

a   Figures in this series are not available for years before 1967.

b   Figures are not available for GNP for 1971.

c   IMF Yearbook does not give a conversion rate from national currency to United

INVISIBLE TRADE: 1960, 1964 and 1971

Invisible Receipts as % of GNP			Invisible Receipts as % of Total Payments			Invisible Payments as % of GNP		
1960	1964	1971	1960	1964	1971	1960	1964	1971
1.6	1.9	2.2	20.3	21.7	22.6	1.0	1.1	1.4
7.7	7.3	8.8	26.2	25.0	30.3	6.3	5.7	6.8
–	–	4.5	–	–	24.5	..	–	4.0
5.5	5.7	6.4	20.0	22.2	25.4	3.4	3.8	5.0
2.7	2.8	3.4	21.6	23.7	27.1	4.1	4.8	5.6
11.3	11.5	–	15.5	16.6	22.4	6.9	7.6	–
7.0	7.0	10.8	17.7	17.8	23.1	6.2	6.9	10.5
22.1	20.9	20.6	31.1	28.9	28.8	14.1	12.7	13.1
10.3	10.2	12.5	16.6	11.7	14.4	5.5	4.2	5.1
6.3	5.2	4.9	15.2	15.5	20.4	4.3	4.1	5.0
5.5	8.3	10.4	13.5	15.7	20.2	3.6	4.2	6.1
7.8	7.2	7.6	15.8	15.7	19.2	5.4	5.2	6.0
4.4	9.1	10.7	12.5	17.7	16.8	3.2	5.9	6.0
3.5	3.7	5.8	11.9	12.9	16.1	2.9	3.1	4.8
3.7	6.3	8.0	17.0	14.1	26.1	1.5	2.0	3.3
3.4	4.0	–	6.9	10.6	16.0	1.7	2.0	–
4.8	5.7	7.0	8.7	9.7	12.6	1.6	2.0	2.6
13.3	13.1	10.3	14.4	14.5	13.0	5.6	6.5	5.7
1.3	1.4	1.8	21.3	24.2	29.2	2.6	3.0	2.7
2.9	3.5	3.6	25.9	26.2	26.6	6.0	6.2	6.3
1.9	2.7	3.0	26.3	26.9	34.4	5.5	5.7	6.5
3.0	2.8	4.8	25.6	23.9	29.5	7.7	7.0	9.2
4.6	4.1	–	28.1	32.3	41.6	3.9	4.1	–
5.0	5.2	4.3	25.4	26.9	26.9	7.2	6.7	14.8
–	–	–	13.2	27.7	25.8	–	–	–
3.1	3.3	4.2	21.2	21.9	25.1	2.6	2.8	3.7
–	–	–	22.0	24.7	18.3	–	–	–
–	–	–	21.4	22.5	23.4	–	–	–

on material collected by the International Monetary Fund.

States dollars because of the continual fluctuation of the peso.

substantial surpluses. (The "rankings" are shown in Table 4 below.) Apart from these, all of the countries of Western Europe have surpluses on invisible account, with the noticeable exception of West Germany, which has a substantial deficit. Among other developed countries, Japan, Canada, Australia and South Africa also have considerable deficits. In addition, the position of countries with respect to their net balances on invisibles tends to be stable over time. Surplus countries tend to stay in surplus; deficit countries, in deficit. This suggests that the factors determining whether a country has a comparative advantage (disadvantage) in invisible trade, and therefore has a surplus (deficit), are difficult to influence over a short period.

Table 3 shows four different measures of the dependence of the leading 25 countries in the world on invisible trade: (a) invisible receipts as a percentage of total receipts from abroad; (b) invisible receipts as a percentage of the domestic gross national product (GNP); (c) invisible payments as a percentage of total payments abroad; and (d) invisible payments as a percentage of domestic GNP. The countries whose balance of payments were most dependent in 1970 on invisibles were Mexico, Spain and Norway, the first due in particular to travel income from the United States. Using the same measure of dependence, next to these were Greece, Yugoslavia, Israel and Britain. If invisible receipts as a percentage of GNP is taken as the measure of a country's dependence on invisible trade, the countries most dependent in 1970 on invisible income were Norway (20.5 per cent), Switzerland (12.5 per cent) and the Netherlands and Ireland (11.6 per cent). For Britain the figure was 8.9 per cent while for the United States it was only 2.2 per cent.

British Invisible Trade

In the particular case of the United Kingdom invisible trade is important in terms of its current account.[12] Britain ranks second in the world to the United States in terms of invisible earnings (see Table 4). In 1968 her receipts from invisible trade were 39 per cent of her receipts from visible trade. Throughout the 1960s this ratio remained extremely stable —

averaging 37 per cent. Invisible receipts as a percentage of GNP were 6.57 per cent in 1970 and between 1960 and 1970 averaged 5.43 per cent. As a percentage of GNP, invisible receipts increased from 5.81 per cent in 1960 to 7.46 per cent in 1970.

Table 4

TOP TEN INVISIBLE EARNERS: 1970 and 1971

($m)

	Total Receipts		% of World Total	
	1970	1971	1970	1971
United States	21,514	23,617	23.2	22.2
United Kingdom	10,858	12,026	11.7	11.3
West Germany	6,278	7,411	6.8	7.0
France	6,047	7,343	6.5	6.9
Italy	5,592	6.475	6.0	6.1
Netherlands	3,728	4,461	4.0	4.2
Japan	3,317	4,195	3.6	3.9
Canada	3,209	3,366	3.5	3.2
Belgium-Luxembourg	2,846	3,150	3.1	3.0
Switzerland	2,569	3,067	2.8	2.9

Source: *World Invisible Trade* (London: Committee on Invisible Exports, 1974), based on material collected by the International Monetary Fund.

Although invisible earnings are extremely important to Britain's balance of payments, her share in total world invisible receipts and payments has been falling gradually. In 1964 Britain's share of world total invisible receipts was 14.6 per cent whereas in 1968 it was 12.0 per cent. Similarly in 1964 the per share of world total invisible payments was 11.8 per cent whereas in 1968 it was only 9.2 per cent. This relative decline in invisible earnings is due to the relatively faster growth of invisible exports by the European Community (as a whole), Japan, Yugoslavia, Mexico, Israel, South Africa and Argentina. The statistics for Britain's balance-of-payments current account and its breakdown into visible and invisible between 1960 and 1970 are given in Table 5. Also see Table 6.

Table 5   INVISIBLES IN THE UNITED KINGDOM'S

	1960	1961	1962	1963	1964
A. VISIBLE TRADE					
1. Exports (f.o.b.)	3,732	3,801	3,993	4,282	4,486
2. Imports (f.o.b.)	4,138	4,043	4,095	4,362	5,005
Visible trade balance (1–2)	– –406	– 152	– 102	– 80	– 519
B. INVISIBLES					
Government services and transfers (Net)	– 282	– 332	– 360	– 382	– 432
Other invisibles Private[a] services and transfers	+ 200	+ 236	+ 250	+ 188	+ 176
Interest, profits and dividends					
Private sector	+ 381	+ 418	+ 480	+ 531	+ 512
Public sector	– 148	– 164	– 146	– 133	– 119
Invisible balance	+ 151	+ 158	+ 224	+ 204	+ 137
CURRENT BALANCE (A+B)	– 255	+ 6	+ 122	+ 124	– 382

Source: Financial Statistics (London: Central Statistical Office, May 1974).

[a] Including public corporations

Table 6   INVISIBLES IN THE UNITED KINGDOM'S

	1955	1956	1957	1958	1959	1960	1961
Gross private invisible receipts[a, b]	1,643	1,817	1,915	2,011	2,019	2,117	2,185
Gross private invisible payments[a, b]	1,347	1,487	1,509	1,336	1,404	1,536	1,531
Net private invisibles[a]	+296	+330	+406	+675	+615	+531	+654
Net government[a] transactions	– 138	– 175	– 144	– 360	– 355	– 430	– 496
Total net invisibles (private & government)	+158	+155	+262	+315	+260	+151	+158
Total visible trade net (exports-imports)	– 313	+53	– 29	+29	– 117	– 406	– 152
Current account balance	– 155	+208	+233	+344	+ 143	– 255	– 6

Source: World Invisible Trade (London: Committee on Invisible Exports, 1973); the London, March 1972.

[a] For 1955-7 inclusive, net Government transactions do not include the public sector actions.

[b] Consisting of interest, profits and dividends, services and transfers.

CURRENT ACCOUNT: 1960-73   ($m)

1965	1966	1967	1968	1969	1970	1971	1972	1973
4,817	5,184	5,124	6,274	7,063	7,893	8,796	9.134	11,435
5,054	5,257	5,681	6,993	7,206	7,902	8,511	9,819	13,810
− 237	− 73	− 557	− 659	− 143	− 9	− 285	− 685	−2,375
− 447	− 470	− 463	− 466	− 467	− 486	− 526	− 548	− 772
+ 200	+ 240	+ 325	+ 506	+ 556	+ 672	+ 786	+ 840	+ 916
+ 569	+ 546	+ 551	+ 571	+ 833	+ 777	+ 715	+ 623	+ 985
− 134	− 159	− 172	− 236	− 334	− 262	− 199	− 147	−222
+ 188	+ 157	+ 241	+ 375	+ 588	+ 701	+ 776	+ 768	+ 907
− 49	+ 84	− 316	− 284	+ 445	+ 692	+1,061	+ 83	−1,468

CURRENT ACCOUNT: 1955-71   ($m)

1962	1963	1964	1965	1966	1967	1968	1969	1970	1971
2,297	2,405	2,558	2,780	2,856	3,146	3,721	4,213	4,790	5,276
1,567	1,686	1,870	2,011	2,070	2,269	2,642	2,825	3,373	3,809
+730	+719	+688	+769	+786	+877	+1,079	+1,388	+1,417	+1,467
−506	−515	−551	−581	−629	−635	−702	−801	−748	−726
+224	+204	+137	+188	+157	+242	+377	+587	+669	+741
−102	−80	−519	−237	−73	−557	−648	−143	+12	+299
+122	+124	−382	−49	+84	−315	−271	+444	+681	+1,040

United Kingdom Balance of Payments, 1971 (the "Pink Book") and *Economic Trends,*

element of interest, profits and dividends. These are included in private invisible trans-

Table 7

ANALYSIS OF INVISIBLES IN THE UNITED KINGDOM'S BALANCE OF PAYMENTS: 1962-72

(£m)

	1962	1963	1964	1965	1966	1967	1968	1969	1970	1971	1972
CREDITS											
Government Services	39	40	45	46	42	36	44	48	51	59	75
Private(1) services											
Transport											
Sea transport	647	658	697	749	765	884	1,053	1,051	1,361	1,609	1,645
Civil aviation	119	131	143	162	180	199	235	287	316	354	410
Travel	183	188	190	193	219	236	282	359	432	489	551
Other services	522	510	558	594	653	766	914	1,042	1,202	1,325	1,516
Total	1,471	1,487	1,588	1,698	1,817	2,055	2,484	2,739	3,311	3,777	4,122
Interest, profits and dividends											
Private sector	715	805	845	947	907	920	1,069	1,299	1,323	1,371	1,418
Public sector	39	37	43	45	55	57	38	39	65	100	167
Total	754	842	588	992	962	977	1,107	1,338	1,388	1,471	1,585
Private transfers	111	113	125	135	135	143	171	181	192	202	211
Total credits	2,375	2,482	2,616	2,871	2,956	3,241	3,806	4,306	4,942	5,509	5,993
DEBTS											
Government services	278	290	314	316	332	311	331	338	365	385	434
Government transfers	121	132	163	177	180	188	-179	177	172	200	189
Total	399	422	477	493	512	499	510	515	537	585	623

Sea transport	666	673	734	748	756	801	902	1,052	1,436	1,668	1,699
Civil aviation	97	104	116	134	150	172	206	246	279	309	346
Travel	210	241	261	290	297	274	271	324	382	437	529
Other services	256	270	291	319	348	369	428	482	508	547	613
Total	1,231	1,294	1,402	1,491	1,555	1,716	1,923	2,134	2,605	2,961	3,187
Int., profits and dvdns.											
Private sector	235	274	333	378	361	369	498	466	546	656	815
Public sector	185	170	162	179	214	229	274	373	327	299	314
Total	420	444	495	557	575	598	772	839	873	955	1,129
Private transfers	101	118	135	142	157	187	226	230	226	232	286
Total debits	2,151	2,278	2,509	2,683	2,799	3,000	3,431	3,718	4,241	4,733	5,225
NET											
Government services	−239	−250	−269	−270	−290	−275	−287	−290	−314	−326	−359
Government transfers	−121	−132	−163	−177	−180	−188	−179	−177	−172	−200	−189
Total	−360	−382	−432	−447	−470	−463	−466	−467	−486	−526	−548
Private (1) services											
Transport											
Sea transport	− 21	− 21	− 37	+ 1	+ 5	− 17	+ 35	− 31	− 75	− 59	− 54
Civil aviation	+ 22	+ 27	+ 27	+ 28	+ 30	+ 27	+ 29	+ 41	+ 37	+ 45	+ 64
Travel	− 27	− 53	− 71	− 97	− 78	− 38	+ 11	+ 35	+ 50	+ 52	+ 22
Other services	+266	+240	+267	+275	+305	+397	+486	+560	+694	+778	+903
Total	+240	+193	+186	+207	+262	+369	+561	+605	+706	+816	+935
Int., profits and dvdns.											
Private sector	+480	+531	+512	+569	+546	+551	+571	+833	+777	+715	+603
Public sector	−146	−133	−119	−134	−159	−172	−236	−334	−262	−199	−147
Total	+334	+398	+393	+435	+387	+379	+335	+499	+515	+516	+456
Private transfers	+ 10	− 5	− 10	− 7	− 22	− 44	− 55	− 49	− 34	− 30	− 75
Invisible balance	+224	+204	+137	+188	+157	+241	+375	+588	+701	+776	+768

(1) Including public corporations

Source: United Kingdom Balance of Payments 1973 (London: Central Statistical Office, 1973)

The basic pattern of a deficit on the visible trade account and a surplus on the invisible account is something which has been true of the United Kingdom's balance of payments throughout the present century. Between 1960 and 1970 the size of the surplus on the invisibles account has increased dramatically from £151m in 1960 to £576m in 1970. The breakdown of invisibles into government services, public and private transfers, private services (such as shipping, civil aviation, travel and "other services") and the payment of interest, profits and dividends (both to and by the government and private sectors) is shown in Table 7. "Other services" is defined to include insurance, banking, merchanting, brokerage, commissions on imports and exports, telecommunications and postal services, films and television, services rendered by and to branches, subsidiaries and associates and other overseas concerns and other minor items.

The first feature which stands out from this table is that throughout the period the public sector has been in substantial deficit, while the private sector has been in even more substantial surplus, so producing an overall surplus on the invisible account as a whole. The average of the public sector deficit between 1960 and 1970 was £599m, ranging from a deficit of £430m in 1960 to a deficit of £798m in 1969. With the exception of 1970, when it was £740m, the size of the deficit increased annually between 1960 and 1970. During the same period, however, the size of the private sector surplus increased even more dramatically. In 1960 the surplus was £581m, while in 1969 it was £1,379m, falling slightly in 1970 to £1,332m. Throughout the period 1960-70 the average size of the surplus was £871m, giving therefore an average net invisible balance throughout the period of £272m.

A second feature of this table is the relative stability of the various private sector type of invisible earnings. Throughout the decade the average ratio of sectoral earnings to total British invisible earnings (gross) was 27 per cent for shipping, 5.75 per cent for civil aviation, 7.7 per cent for travel, 22.2 per cent for other services and 29.1 per cent for the interest, profits and dividends of private sector direct and portfolio foreign investment. Civil aviation showed a steady growth from 4.4 per cent in 1960 to 6.5 per cent in 1970. Travel was much the same proportionally throughout the period. Shipping receipts as a proportion of invisible earnings varied more than any other item largely as a result of cyclical variations in shipping rates, changing for example from 24.5 per cent to 28.2 per cent in just one year (1970) although the total range of variation was only from 24.5 per cent to 29.1 per cent. Other services again showed considerable stability ranging only from 20.6 per cent to 24.0 per cent.

Growth of World Capital Markets

Alongside the expansion of invisible trade over the late 1960s and early 1970s has been a remarkable growth in the development of world capital markets, which has had important repercussions for restrictions on international movements of capital. The same period has seen the dollar become

(a) the world's money in that it has become the unit of account for measuring prices and incomes internationally,

(b) the world's standard of deferred payment for the issuance of securities, and

(c) the store of value, albeit reluctantly toward the end of the 1960s, and the means of payment.

Any capital market brings together individuals, companies, institutions and governments who wish to borrow and lend funds at certain prices (interest rates), over varying time periods and subject to certain conditions.

The capital markets which have developed deal in funds that vary in their maturity from overnight money and short-term deposits (Euro-currency markets) to medium-term bank lending and medium and long-term bonds (international bond markets).[13] Euro-currencies are those currencies foreign to a particular country, but in which domestic banks typically borrow and lend. For British banks such currencies would be any other than sterling. The most important Euro-currency market is the Euro-dollar market. International bonds are bonds sold outside the country of the issuer and are usually classified as Euro-bonds and foreign

Table 8

EXTERNAL LIABILITIES AND CLAIMS OF BANKS IN THE UNITED KINGDOM IN NON-STERLING CURRENCIES: 1963-73

(£m)

LIABILITIES

End of Period	1963	1964	1965	1966	1967	1968	1969	1970	1971	1972	1973
Overseas sterling countries	41	82	125	200	298	546	1,049	1,280	1,365	2,285	3,843
United States	153	204	195	349	588	1,119	1,270	1,280	1,297	1,530	2,113
Canada	133	273	170	201	324	505	1,087	1,277	1,386	1,764	2,127
Latin America	67	90	100	135	201	276	575	735	980	1,772	2,374
Western Europe	652	850	1,165	1,692	2,413	3,917	6,709	9,045	10,457	14,327	9,737
Middle East	131	159	215	234	231	235	286	457	707	1,415	1,797
Japan	4	7	10	11	16	26	127	169	297	500	1,234
Other[a]	99	121	142	180	313	515	891	910	1,121	1,867	3,186
European Economic Community	–	–	–	–	–	–	–	–	–	–	12,606
TOTAL	1,280	1,786	2,122	3,002	4,384	7,139	11,994	15,153	17,610	25,460	39,017
Of which:											
United States dollars	1,072	1,566	1,893	2,727	4,038	6,404	10,728	13,086	14,172	20,539	29,770
Other currencies	208	220	229	275	346	735	1,266	2,067	3,438	4,921	9,247
Deutschemarks	65	83	96	104	128	346	615	1,154	1,995	2,522	5,126
Swiss Francs	76	83	72	109	118	242	454	676	1,046	1,658	2,943

CLAIMS

End of Period	1963	1964	1965	1966	1967	1968	1969	1970	1971	1972	1973
Overseas sterling countries	3	4	24	39	99	177	554	940	2005	3629	5683
United States	290	435	575	1244	1710	3061	5617	4151	2032	2306	3011
Canada	37	26	55	93	145	202	267	377	475	900	1413
Latin America	29	30	76	81	177	342	616	899	1309	2096	3057
Western Europe	692	840	916	1161	1453	2166	3570	6270	8167	11165	3923
Middle East	17	31	42	49	87	124	130	212	201	290	431
Japan	127	181	209	249	451	695	675	1021	1305	1914	3093
Other a	73	79	83	104	254	350	577	821	1226	1719	3145
European Economic Community	–	–	–	–	–	–	–	–	–	–	12518
TOTAL	1,268	1,626	1,980	3,020	4,376	7,117	12,006	14,691	16,720	24,019	36,274
Of which:											
United States dollars	1,024	1,312	1,624	2,611	3,837	6,245	10,514	12,189	13,104	19,422	28,174
Other currencies	244	314	356	409	539	872	1,492	2,502	3,616	4,597	8,100
Deutschemarks	68	119	162	167	224	441	795	1,363	1,955	2,500	4,403
Swiss francs	71	85	81	94	148	246	496	868	1,341	1,540	2,829

Source: Bank of England *Statistical Abstract*, Vol 1 (London: 1970) and Bank of England *Quarterly Bulletin* (London: June 1974).

a Includes unallocated items; under liabilities these are mainly unallocated dollar certificates of deposit which are thought to be held by residents of non-sterling countries.

Table 9

GROWTH OF EURO-CURRENCY MARKETS: 1966-71

($m)

End of Month	Dollars		Other Foreign Currencies						
	Total	of which Non-banks	Total	of which Non-banks	Deutsche Mark	Swiss Francs	Sterling	Guilders	All other Foreign Currencies
LIABILITIES									
1966 December	14,770	4,130	3,690	610	970	1,220	710	70	720
1967 June	14,930	4,090	4,290	510	1,470	1,300	950	90	480
1967 December	18,120	4,660	4,330	470	1,670	1,400	800	100	360
1968 June	22,360	6,390	9,600	700	2,180	2,030	1,020	120	450
1968 December	26,970	6,240	6,890	1,040	3,010	2,200	800	250	540
1969 March	29,860	7,600	7,670	930	3,060	2,800	900	280	630
1969 June	37,960	8,600	9,450	1,320	4,260	3,290	910	340	650
1969 September	41,540	9,960	10,240	1,340	4,800	3,700	760	240	650
1969 December	46,200	10,400	10,630	1,320	4,640	4,030	810	350	800
1970 March	46,050	11,100	11,420	1,370	4,430	4,900	970	350	710
1970 June	49,440	11,000	13,090	1,660	5,550	5,360	940	410	830
1970 September	50,230	10,770	15,190	2,810	6,830	5,740	940	550	1,130
1970 December	56,700	11,240	16,590	2,450	8,060	5,720	940	550	1,300
1971 March	59,500	11,120	18,000	2,530	9,360	5,250	1,320	450	1,620
1971 June	61,920	10,910	20,400	3,110	11,350	5,670	1,420	490	1,490
1971 September	62,430	9,380	22,650	2,700	12,380	6,730	1,460	510	1,670
1971 December	70,820	9,980	27,110	2,750	14,890	7,760	2,110	860	1,490
ASSETS									
1966 December	16,070	2,100	4,150	690	1,420	360	500	170	860
1967 June	16,580	2,550	4,870	810	1,670	830	1,340	200	830
1967 December	19,690	6,480	4,960	850	2,000	1,110	870	230	600
1968 June	25,560	4,320	5,800	1,340	2,730	1,570	600	280	710
1968 December	29,430	5,150	7,400	1,500	3,920	1,020	610	290	700

1968 March	33,650	5,230	7,440	1,670	4,020	1,850	580	250	720
1969 June	42,260	5,940	9,190	2,030	5,380	2,010	670	310	810
1969 September	44,820	6,110	10,820	2,620	6,980	2,240	630	240	780
1969 December	47,530	6,090	10,600	2,100	5,990	2,980	580	370	770
1970 March	48,970	9,760	11,700	2,470	8,270	3,490	880	340	780
1970 June	52,030	8,550	13,100	2,980	6,830	3,920	710	470	1,140
1970 September	52,930	9,890	15,470	3,940	8,140	4,540	540	550	1,800
1970 December	60,370	11,850	17,880	4,670	10,110	5,080	610	560	1,520
1971 March	62,460	13,380	10,220	5,500	11,440	4,500	930	490	1,060
1971 June	55,060	14,040	20,750	5,960	12,430	5,000	950	510	1,840
1971 September [a]	62,440	13,820	23,010	6,850	13,680	6,420	1,200	480	2,130
1971 December	71,720	14,300	28,600	8,750	15,180	8,100	1,620	700	2,030

NET POSITION

1966 December	1,300	− 2,030	490	180	450	− 290	90	100	140
1967 June	1,650	− 1,440	590	300	200	− 470	390	110	350
1967 December	1,770	− 1,250	620	380	390	− 200	70	130	330
1968 June	3,180	− 2,070	90	640	550	− 450	420	160	250
1968 December	3,560	− 1,090	510	450	910	− 470	190	40	220
1969 March	3,770	− 2,370	− 230	740	950	− 950	310	30	100
1969 June	4,320	− 2,750	− 270	710	1,120	− 1,200	240	30	100
1969 September	3,280	− 3,850	580	1,180	2,130	− 1,550	130	−	80
1969 December	1,430	− 4,370	60	840	1,350	− 1,050	230	20	30
1970 March	920	− 4,340	340	1,100	1,840	− 1,470	90	10	70
1970 June	2,590	− 2,440	10	1,320	1,300	− 1,430	200	60	310
1970 September	3,700	− 880	280	1,630	1,310	− 1,260	300	−	470
1970 December	1,970	610	1,290	2,220	2,080	− 640	300	10	220
1971 March	2,860	2,260	1,220	3,060	2,080	− 760	390	40	240
1971 June	3,150	3,130	350	2,850	1,120	− 670	470	20	350
1971 September [a]	1,010	4,450	1,280	3,650	1,000	− 310	260	30	550
1971 December	900	4,380	1,580	4,000	1,270	− 420	490	180	540

Source: 42nd Annual Report, Bank for International Settlements, Basle, June 1972

a New duties as from September 1971

Table 11

NEW ISSUES OF INTERNATIONAL BONDS IN NORTH AMERICA AND WESTERN EUROPE, 1963- mid-1971[1]

($m)

Borrower	1963	1964	1965	1966	1967	1968	1969	1970	1st Half[2] 1971
Issued in the United States	1,392	1,310	1,689	1,654	2,170	2,014	1,336	1,293	809
Canada	791	850	1,064	1,239	1,344	1,259	1,091	795	277
Other developed countries	536	102	203	36	42	60	10	–	–
Less developed countries	65	208	222	204	274	225	235	198	82
International institutions	–	150	200	175	510	470	–	300	450
Issued in Canada	–	4	30	37	–	17	1	–	–
TOTAL issued in North America	1,392	1,314	1,719	1,692	2,170	2,031	1,337	1,293	809
Issued in Europe									
Developed countries	478	831	1,076	1,332	1,885	4,274	3,757	3,409	2,489
EEC	187	198	250	280	406	432	934	1,138	583
Belgium-Luxembourg	54	85	69	52	74	31	190	19	–
France	33	20	43	27	157	124	186	267	225
Germany	49	37	30	79	58	9	229	127	64
Italy	40	30	80	60	73	84	119	433	136
Netherlands	11	6	28	62	44	184	210	292	158
United Kingdom	16	15	48	52	74	149	283	258	265
Scandinavian countries	75	322	210	93	210	246	238	300	283
Canada	–	–	–	–	16	485	335	178	77
Japan	59	189	35	–	–	179	261	120	70
Other developed countries	119	85	168	216	456	316	429	309	481
Europe	29	43	35	107	190	138	219	92	198

Australia, New Zealand and S. Africa	90	42	133	109	266	178	210	217	283
US companies	9	–	341	629	598	2,433	1,257	1,092	687
Multinational Corporations[3]	13	22	24	62	125	34	20	15	43
Less developed countries	24	16	15	74	173	307	154	144	–
International Institutions	172	433	428	658	619	1,117	970	1,177	708
International development	100	223	312	373	345	908[4]	865	962[5]	463[6]
Multilateral European	72	210	116	285	274	209	105	215	245
TOTAL issued in Europe	674	1,280	1,518	2,064	2,677	5,698	4,881	4,731	3,197
Of which									
European bonds	269	650	640	627	539	1,963	1,600	1,011	–
Euro-bonds	405	630	878	1,437	2,138	3,935	3,281	3,720	–
GRAND TOTAL	2,066	2,594	3,237	3,756	4,847	7,729	6,218	6,024	4,006

Source: International Bank for Reconstruction and Development.

1 Includes issues both publicly offered and privately placed.

2 Preliminary.

3 Includes the following corporations: Acieries Réunies de Burbach-Eich-Dudelange, Americas Holdings SA, BFC Finance, NV, NV Rotterdam-Rijn Pijleiding, Shell Finance Company, NV, Shell International Finance NV, Société Financière Européenne and Trans-alpine Finance Holdings.

4 Includes the following issues by the IBRD: one issue of KD 15.0 million publicly offered in Korea and two issues totalling $30.0 million privately placed in Saudi Arabia.

5 Includes the following issues: one issue of LL 10.0 million privately placed in the Libyian Arab Republic by the IBRD, one issue of Y 6.0 billion publicly offered in Japan by the Asian Development Bank, and two issues totalling Y 72.0 billion privately placed in Japan by the IBRD.

6 Includes the following issues by the IBRD: one issue of Y 11.0 billion publicly offered in Japan and three issues totalling Y 79.0 billion privately placed in Japan.

bonds. The basis of the classification is that Euro-bonds are underwritten by an international syndicate and sold in a number of countries and foreign bonds are underwritten by a national banking syndicate outside the issuer's country and sold mainly in the country to which that syndicate belongs.

Growth in Euro-currency markets is shown in Table 8. Between December 1963 and December 1971, and measured in terms of liabilities of British banks, the Euro-dollar market which is by far the largest of the Euro-currency markets, grew from £652m to £17,610m. In 1970 in particular, the growth of the market was particularly large, by just over 25 per cent. The growth of the Euro-dollar market measured in terms of the liabilities of all banks outside the United States is shown in Table 9. The growth of other Euro-currency

Table 10

FOREIGN BOND ISSUES:[a] 1958-68

($m)

| | Foreign Issues on Domestic Markets | | International | |
	United States	European[d]	Issues[b]	Total
1958	1,138	302	82	1,522
1959	802	337	31	1,170
1960	636	393	29	1,058
1961	558	559	79	1,196
1962	1,185	430	–	1,615
1963	1,414	426	119	1,958
1964	1,191	263	838	2,293
1965	1,532	264 [c]	1,192	2,989
1966	1,317	550 [c]	1,155	3,021
1967	1,619	404 [c]	2,002	4,025
1968	1,576	1,185 [c]	3,517	6,278

Source: Richard N. Cooper, "Towards an International Capital Market", in Charles P. Kindleberger and Andrew Shonfield (eds), *North American and Western European Economic Policies* (London: Macmillan, for the International Economic Association, 1971). The table is compiled from data obtained from 1958-66 OECD Capital Markets Study, *Functioning of Capital Markets* (Paris: OECD, 1968), p. 717; 1967-8 Department of Commerce, *Survey of Current Business* and Morgan Guaranty Trust Company, *World Financial Markets*, New York.

[a]   Including private placements and convertible bonds.

[b]   Foreign bonds issued in Germany after imposition of the 25 per cent coupon tax on German bonds in March 1964 are treated as international issues, since they are exempt from the tax.

[c]   Including the Canadian market.

[d]   Excludes portion purchased by foreigners.

markets is also shown in the table. These statistics, which are derived from the Bank of International Settlements, are the best available.

The growth of the international bond market, while not so phenomenal, is nevertheless substantial. Table 10 shows the growth of foreign bond issues between 1958-68, from $1,522m to $6,278m, and Table 11 shows the growth 1963-9 in a more detailed way. The rapid growth of these markets is integral to understanding the attempts by countries to impose short-term controls on the international flow of capital.

NOTES

1. Percy Bidwell, *The Invisible Tariff* (New York: Council on Foreign Relations, 1939).
2. Geoffrey Denton and Seamus O'Cleireacain, *Subsidy Issues in International Commerce*, Thames Essay No. 5 (London: Trade Policy Research Centre, 1972), pp. 2-4.
3. Such transactions do not record the movement in direct capital. The establishment of a branch abroad of a bank, for instance, would be recorded as an outflow on the capital account. It would not be recorded in the invisibles section of the current account.
4. See, for instance, *Twenty Second Annual Report on Exchange Restrictions* (Washington: International Monetary Fund, 1971); and *Derogations to the OECD Codes of Liberalization of Capital Movements and Current Invisible Operations* (Paris: OECD Secretariat, 1971).
5. "Flag Discrimination", Annex V in *Non-tariff Obstacles to Trade* (Paris: International Chamber of Commerce, 1969).
6. "Details of Main Provisions Involving Flag Discrimination in Force or Contemplated by Certain Countries", Appendix 4 to the *Report of the Committee of Enquiry into Shipping*, Rochdale Report, Cmnd. 4337 (London: HM Stationery Office, 1970); and the report by UNCTAD, *Study on Insurance Legislation and Supervision in Developing Countries*, TD/B/C.3/84, TD/B/C.3/AC.5/1 (New York: United Nations, 1971).
7. For a breakdown of invisibles, see Eduardo Merigo and Stephen Potter, "Invisibles in the 1960s", *OECD Economic Outlook*, OECD Secretariat, Paris, July 1970.
8. In the United Kingdom, net earnings from abroad do *not* include earnings on services rendered by British financial institutions to related enterprises abroad or to profits of overseas branches, subsidiaries and associates of British financial institutions. These are

included under respectively "services rendered to related concerns and interest, profits and dividends".

9. The same applies here as in note 6 above.
10. For an analysis of international trade in invisibles, see *World Invisible Trade* (London: Committee on Invisible Exports, 1975).
11. The discrepancy between the two measures is partly accounted for by normal statistical errors or reporting delays and partly by differences in the classification of transactions.
12. See Thomas Bland *et al.*, *Britain's Invisible Earnings*, Report of the Committee on Invisible Exports (London: British National Export Council, 1967). The director of the study was William M. Clarke.
13. For a detailed account of the growth of these markets, see Richard N. Cooper, "Towards an International Capital Market?", in Charles P. Kindleberger and Andrew Schonfield (eds), *North American and Western European Economic Policies* (London: Macmillan, for the International Economic Association, 1971); *Annual Report*, 1970 (Washington: International Monetary Fund, 1970) and the 1971 annual report; and David Williams, "Foreign Currency Issues in European Security Markets", *IMF Staff Papers*, International Monetary Fund, Washington, May 1967.

CHAPTER 2

Analysis of Barriers to Invisible Trade

The attempt to classify invisibles into particular categories, as was done in the previous chapter, follows closely the definitions of the IMF and those given in the official British balance-of-payments statistics. From an economic point of view, such a classification, and the resulting concept of an "invisibles" section in the balance-of-payments account, is not particularly useful. For it fails to distinguish between (i) the flow of currently-produced services, (ii) the movement of capital which is the source of those services, (iii) the earnings of direct foreign investment concerned with the production of goods and (iv) interest payments on short-term capital movements.

A more useful distinction would be between the flow of currently-produced services and the movement of capital.

Flow of Current Services

All transactions in services between private residents of say the United Kingdom, on the one hand, and government and overseas residents, on the other — again including both the private and public — are classified as services. From an economic viewpoint, it is important to distinguish between financial, transport, government and other services and travel because the factors which affect both the demand and supply of these five types of services are quite different and the types of constraints which are applied by governments also differ. Transport, which is mainly shipping and civil aviation, needs in particular to be differentiated because of the relatively high capital intensity of providing shipping and air services. It also needs to be differentiated because important aspects of both international shipping and air transport are organized so as to reduce price competition through the system of liner conferences and the International Air Transport Association (IATA).

The different types of constraints on international competition in the provision of services are analysed in general terms later in this chapter. But it might be as well to deal straight away, if only briefly, with the specific nature of international transport arrangements since they are often characterized as cartels.

In certain industries firms seek to protect themselves from the rigours of price competition by means of inter-firm agreements which limit competition, divide the available market, pool research and purchasing facilities, adopt common attitudes towards advertising or after-sales service and engage in exclusive dealing arrangements, either by refusal to sell or by refusal to buy. Such agreements tend to be very unstable over long periods of time. If the cartel sets its prices too high, they will attract new entrants to the industry; and, in any case, there will be an incentive for individual firms to "chisel" away at the agreement and so improve their profitability.

By definition, restrictive business agreements – in the field of transport as elsewhere – are negotiated and maintained primarily in the interests of producers, traders and distributors, rather than in the interests of consumers. Such practices are treated in most inter-governmental organizations as a potential threat, if nothing more, to the proper working of competition. Such is the case in the European Community, and in the European Free Trade Association (EFTA), let alone the Organization for Economic Co-operation and Development (OECD) which embraces the developed countries.[1]

As in pleas for protection from import competition, a "special case" is usually made for a restrictive business practice, its plausibility depending very often on non-economic considerations. In the liberalization of international trade that has taken place since the end of the Second World War, agriculture has been placed in a "special position", because it is said to be "different" from other industries. Subsidies to shipbuilding are justified all round the world on the grounds that other countries subsidize their shipbuilding industries. When an industry is isolated from international market forces, the price mechanism ceases to operate effectively and, in the end, it is not surprising that the allocation of resources, both domestically and internationally, becomes grossly distorted — as in agriculture and shipbuilding. That is what is meant by protective government intervention leading inevitably to inefficiency in an economic sense.

In favour of the system of liner conferences, it is argued that, given the nature of the shipping industry, involving large capital commitments and fluctuating market conditions, shipowners could not otherwise provide a regular service of speed and quality. Similar arguments are deployed by the member airlines of IATA which seeks to regulate air routes and fares. The effectiveness of the latter, however, is being constantly undermined by "package tours" and "excursion" and other concessionary fares, not to mention the lower fares offered by non-IATA airlines.

Movement of Capital

The movement of capital, which is the source of currently-produced services, is also classified an an invisible transaction and is further broken down to include both direct investment and portfolio investment.

Direct Investment

Direct investment income relates not only to the net income from, say, British industrial firms in other countries and foreign manufacturing firms in the United Kingdom. It also relates to the net income of British oil companies and foreign oil companies which operate in Britain and the net income from British banks abroad and foreign banks in the United Kingdom. This last item is important. For it is necessary to distinguish carefully in the field of banking and insurance between services performed for non-residents domestically, on the one hand, and services performed by overseas branches, subsidiaries and associates of British companies which give rise to profits overseas, on the other. The former is properly included under services, whereas the latter is comparable to any other income from direct foreign investment.

It is important, too, to distinguish between restrictions which are placed on the flow of interest, profits and dividends between countries and restrictions which are placed on the operation of foreign companies and financial institutions in various countries, which will in turn have a repercussion on the flow of profits and dividends between countries.

Portfolio Investment

As with direct investment, it is still necessary to separate problems connected with the remission of earnings on foreign financial assets between one country and another from those connected with the attempts of countries to restrict the inflow and outflow of portfolio capital. Any discussion of restrictions on the flows of capital between countries must of necessity involve consideration of the workings of the present international monetary system and a country's ability to pursue an independent monetary policy. The growth, in the 1960s, of a world short-term capital market[2] has added a new dimension to these problems.

Types of Constraints

The major distinction which must be made in considering the various constraints on invisible earnings is between:

(a) restrictions which are imposed generally on all persons and/or companies and/or financial institutions in a particular sector of the national economy, but which *do not discriminate*, either in law or in effect between national and foreign enterprises; and

(b) restrictions imposed on foreign enterprises which discriminate against them in favour of domestic competitors.

For example, banking practice in most countries requires that a certain proportion of bank assets be held in specified forms, ones which pay a lower rate of interest than the banks might earn if free to dispose of their funds at will. While such measures may reduce the profitability of British banks abroad, and reduce in turn the United Kingdom's invisible earnings, they usually apply to all banks registered under that particular banking legislation. But if a particular country insisted that foreign banks should hold a greater proportion of their lower-yielding assets in a particular form, not required of domestic banks, the measure would be discriminatory. *It is restrictions that discriminate against foreign interests that are the preoccupation of this study.*

In order to secure some idea of the nature of the constraints on invisible earnings, a survey of the main fields was conducted, although with limited resources it was necessarily restricted in scope. Some information was obtained from primary sources, but the bulk was secured from published material. In Appendix 1 an illustrative list of measures is provided, divided between five areas of activity: banking, direct investment, insurance, shipping and travel. The countries covered are divided between OECD members and the Third World. It should be emphasized, here as in the appendix itself, that the list is by no means comprehensive; it does nothing more than indicate the kind of measures that are found to discriminate in favour of domestic interests and against non-nationals. It is merely illustrative of a general state of affairs.

FINANCIAL AND TRANSPORT SERVICES

Having emphasized the distinction between the flow of currently-produced services and the movement of capital, which is the source of those services, this section will deal with the first, discussing those measures which are explicitly discriminatory against foreign-produced services and also those which, while having wider objectives, nevertheless have discriminatory side effects.

Restriction of Foreign Competition

The most drastic step that a country can take to protect a particular industry — be it shipping, banking, insurance or any other service — is the total and direct exclusion of foreign competition from the provision of that service. This can be achieved either by passing a law which reserves the provision of the service solely to domestic companies, or by maintaining a system of licenses and then being thoroughly exclusive over their allocation, or by imposing a tariff on foreign-produced services sufficiently high to ensure that domestic industry can satisfy the local market at a lower price, or by an outright takeover of foreign companies in the particular area concerned, or by outright nationalization.

Economic Analysis

The effect of such measures is to raise the domestic price of the protected services above the world price and thereby encourage within the country either the development or expansion of the services concerned. The growth of these industries is inefficient in that they are using the scarce labour and capital resources which could be more productively employed elsewhere in the economy. To the extent that domestic prices are different from world prices, this will also lead to a distortion of the demand for these services; for, as a result of the relatively higher domestic prices, less of the services will be demanded than would otherwise be the case. On the other hand, to the extent that domestic prices are not different from world prices, because of the existence of subsidies, such a distortion in demand will not occur.

There is also a balance-of-payments effect. At a given exchange rate, the country may improve in the short term its balance-of-payments position through the pursuit of protective policies, depending on the effect on the terms of trade of alternative uses of the resources. From the viewpoint of exporting countries such actions as these are bound to lead to a reduction in both the volume and value of their exports.

Practice

Examples of attempts totally to exclude foreign competition may be found in the various bilateral agreements of Latin American countries (especially Brazil), as well as in those between India and the Soviet Union, designed to ensure that goods traded between them are carried in the vessels of either country — if there are sufficient available. In insurance there is legislation in Argentina, Bolivia, Columbia, Jordan, Mexico, Senegal and Uruguay which prohibit the insuring abroad of domestic property, the insuring of persons resident in the country or the insuring of risks which may be incurred within the country. Then there are laws reserving a country's coastal trade to national flag ships, as is the case in Brazil, Chile, India and the United States. And in civil aviation most countries reserve internal routes to domestic airlines.

Government Procurement

Most countries practise discrimination in favour of national producers when it comes to the purchase by the government sector of those services which are included under the term invisibles.

Economic Analysis

The effects of such discrimination depend on the marginal costs of providing those services in different countries.[3] If the domestic producer of a particular service is relatively inefficient by comparison with producers from other countries, this means that the government is artificially maintaining the size of that particular industry by providing what is in effect a subsidy. Less of that service will be demanded domestically because of its higher price relative to the world market price and the exports of those countries which produce the service more efficiently will be reduced. If, on the other hand, the domestic producer of that particular service is relatively efficient by world standards, no such allocative distortions are created by the government's procurement policy and there is no artificial restriction on the exports of other countries producing that service. To the extent that the price of the domestically-produced service is the same as the world price, such a policy would mean that the private sector would increase their demand for imports of all goods and services.

Practice

Although it is difficult to know the extent of discriminatory government procurement policies, certain cases — for example, the 1954 Cargo Preference Act in the United States which reserves a minimum of 50 per cent of government cargo to privately-owned American flag ships — are unambiguous.

Exchange Control

A general form of control, imposed by both developed and developing countries, is the various restrictions on domestic residents' ability to purchase foreign exchange in order to enable them to buy foreign-produced services.[4] These restrictions take many specific forms: an outright ban on the purchase of foreign currency other than for officially approved purchases; an allowance to purchase an amount of foreign currency from the government for certain purposes, which is then allocated among users on the basis of price, and usually at a premium (investment currency market); and the practice of multiple exchange rates.

Economic Analysis

The effect of exchange control imposed by countries is to reduce those countries' effective demand for invisible exports from the rest of the world and to raise the demand for domestically-produced financial and transport services. If the marginal resource cost of domestically-produced services is greater than that of internationally-produced services, the domestic service will expand in an inefficient range of production, with the usual misallocative resource effects.

If restrictions are placed on the ability of domestic residents to purchase foreign exchange, the consequences suggested in the previous paragraph are reversed. There is a reduction in the demand for foreign-produced services, a substitution between home and foreign-produced services, a reduction in invisible imports and, depending on the relative costs of producing foreign and domestic services, repercussions on the allocation of resources.

Practice

The most general example of exchange control in the field of services is the restriction on the amount of foreign exchange which may be bought for the purpose of foreign travel. Restrictions of varying degrees are, or have been, in effect in Algeria, Chile, France, Greece, Israel, Nigeria, Peru, Uruguay and the United Kingdom. By contrast with those of other developed countries, Britain's exchange-control practices are very strict, to an extent which can hardly be justified in terms of exchange-rate flexibility.

MOVEMENT OF CAPITAL

The analysis above examined those measures which discriminate against foreign services. But the study is also concerned with measures which discriminate against foreign capital movements and have discriminatory side effects.

DIRECT INVESTMENT

Capital movements are classified under direct investment and portfolio investment. Direct investment here refers to such items as earnings from overseas branches of domestic companies and interest payments for loans granted to subsidiaries and dividends paid by them. The earnings of oil companies, though, are not covered in this study.

Restriction of Foreign Competition

Many countries prohibit the establishment of foreign companies in certain sectors. Some prohibitions are rather stringent: for example, foreign insurance companies are not allowed to operate in Peru. Other constraints are less drastic although they still constitute hindrances.

Foreign companies are not allowed to establish themselves in the United States in fresh water shipping, domestic radio communication and domestic air transport. Ghana excludes foreign companies from certain retail, wholesale and transportation operations. Foreign banks are excluded from

Algeria, Australia, Canada, Tanzania, Turkey and various states in the United States (the most important being Illinois). And foreign insurance companies are excluded from certain areas of business in Mexico and Venezuela.

Constraints on Choice of Product Mix

Less dramatic attempts to protect domestic business against foreign competition are the various constraints placed on the freedom of foreign firms to choose the particular combinations of products they would prefer to produce.

Economic Analysis

In the provision of financial services constraints on product mix take the form of attempts to influence the allocation or portfolio of assets which financial institutions hold, such as specifying the minimum ratio of loans to the public sector in relation to total assets or, within the total of loans granted to the private sector, of specifying the maximum proportion that may be lent for consumption, imports and manufacturing and the minimum proportion that may be lent for exports, investment and agriculture. In the field of transport, constraints take the form of specifying the proportion of business which may be done by domestic and foreign companies respectively. Such constraints must lead to a fall in the short-run profitability of the foreign companies concerned. Unless there are external effects which produce a divergence between the private and social profitability of producing these services, constraints of this nature will lead to a distortion of domestic prices and interest rates and a reduction in the level of real income.

Practice

One activity where constraints on product mix are prevalent is in shipping where discriminatory measures are often applied against foreign operators over special credit and foreign currency terms. Pakistan, Indonesia and Ghana, for example,

while not excluding foreign competition completely, nevertheless seek to reduce its share of the trade.

Constraints on Choice of Factor-Input Mix

A third type of constraint is a restriction which takes the
form of specifying the minimum amounts of certain factors
of production, such as capital and local labour, that must be
employed in the production of certain services.

Economic Analysis

An example of this type of constraint is the regulation that a
minimum amount of local labour be employed or a given
ratio between domestic and foreign employees be maintained. If the two types of labour are perfect substitutes, or if
they are not perfect substitutes but there is an available
supply of skilled local labour, then such a requirement would
have no effect on the output of the firms concerned. If the
two types of labour, however, are complementary, the
restriction that a certain number of persons from the local
labour market must be employed leads to a reduction in the
output of these firms. In the field of banking certain host
countries specify that a foreign bank shall employ a minimum number or percentage of its management from the local
labour market. If managers possessing the right experience
and skill are not available then the number of branches of
foreign banks has to be reduced.

Practice

This policy is applied, among other places, in the Caribbean
— especially Trinidad — towards foreign banks in which there
is a strong demand for them to employ local nationals even
though this may result in a reduction in the amount of
services supplied by the banking sector.

PORTFOLIO INVESTMENT

Classified under capital movements are direct investment and portfolio investment. Portfolio investment relates to such items as credits, which include dividends and interest paid to domestic residents by companies and governments abroad, and debits which are interest and dividends on domestic company securities and domestic public-sector stocks that are held by residents of other countries.

Control of Interest Payments on Deposits

Restrictions in respect of the maximum interest rates which banks and non-banks may pay on foreign-owned deposits are usually imposed to reduce inflows of short-term capital by making the rate of return on deposits placed in the domestic country relatively less than in other countries.[5] The effects of such a regulation would be to reduce the possibilities of substitution between domestic and foreign assets and so isolate domestic interest rate levels from those of the rest of the world. In May 1971 the payment of interest in West Germany on foreign-held deposits exceeding 50,000 marks was made subject to authorization which had been customarily withheld. Similarly, in Switzerland, the Swiss Bankers Association agreed in July 1971 that they would not pay interest on foreign funds held in Swiss franc accounts after that time. In August 1971 the Bank of England imposed the requirement that banks could not pay interest on sterling balances in excess of those held at that time.

Restraints on Foreign Borrowing and Lending

The objective of placing a ceiling on the amount of funds which domestic residents may either lend to foreigners or borrow from abroad is to reduce the amount of capital inflow or outflow associated with an underlying surplus or deficit on the current account. These restraints may be either voluntary or statutory. The effectiveness of such restrictions in reducing an outflow or an inflow of capital depends on the extent to which individuals and companies are able to devise ways of circumventing the official regulations. To the extent that the restraints are binding, their effect will be to isolate the capital markets of a particular country from the rest of the world and in particular to reduce the dependence of domestic on foreign interest rates.

There are numerous examples of such controls. Voluntary foreign credit restraint programmes in the United States have from time to time laid down "guide lines" for the foreign lending of banks and other financial institutions. There was for a while a statutory Foreign Direct Investment Programme in the United States. Credit granted by Mexican banks to subsidiaries of foreign companies in Mexico is subject to guide lines which are drawn up by the Mexican Bankers Association and which apply to companies with assets of over 3m Mexican dollars and are more than 15 per cent foreign owned. France maintains special controls on both borrowing and lending abroad. Malawi, Trinidad and Tobago, Jamaica and Venezuela have restrictions on local borrowing by non-resident controlled companies.

Fiscal Measures

Countries may also use fiscal measures to attempt to regulate the net flow of capital. American citizens or residents who purchase foreign stocks and debt obligations from foreigners are subject to an interest equalization tax which is equivalent to a borrowing charge of 0.75 per cent per year. The tax, which was introduced in 1963, has been designed to reduce the domestic demand for foreign-issued debt by equalizing the rate of return on foreign and United States domestic issued debt. Between 1964-1971, West Germany imposed a special withholding tax on the interest paid to foreign holders of domestic bonds, making it the equivalent of a negative interest equalization tax. Foreign debt which is issued in West Germany, however, is exempt from the tax, so that it carries a lower yield than domestic debt and is therefore an incentive to attract borrowers from abroad.

Reserve Requirements

Some countries make the bank deposits of non-residents subject to higher reserve ratios than those of residents. The Bundesbank in West Germany introduced such higher re-

serves for the first time from May 1957 to March 1959 and
again from February 1961 to January 1962, from April 1964
to January 1967 and from June to October 1969. In
addition the Bundesbank has sometimes fixed special minimum reserve requirements for any increase in non-resident
bank deposits. Such requirements were applied from January
1960 to April 1961, from December 1963 to October 1969,
from April to August 1970 and have been in force since
December 1970.

Since December 1971, West Germany has made the foreign
borrowings of non-banking institutions subject to minimum
reserve requirements of up to 50 per cent.[6] They are:

Reserve class	Banking institutions with liabilities subject to reserves of:	Liabilities at sight	Time deposits	Savings deposits
1	DM 1,000m plus	31.7	22	16.2
2	DM 100m–1,000m	29.3	19.5	16.2
3	DM 10m–100m	26.8	17.1	16.2
4	DM 10m	24.4	14.6	14.6

Exchange Control

Various countries attempt to control the inflow and outflow
of portfolio capital, not through particular devices such as
those mentioned above, but through control of foreign
exchange. With the exception of nineteen countries (Afghani-
stan, Belgium-Luxembourg, Bolivia, Canada, Costa Rica,
Germany, Honduras, Hong Kong, Indonesia, Kuwait, Laos,
Lebanon, Liberia, Mexico, Nicaragua, Panama, Saudi Arabia
and the United States) all other members of the International
Monetary Fund, approximately 100, have restrictions on
payments with respect to capital movements.

CONSTRAINTS IN PARTICULAR FIELDS

As part of the study, an attempt was made to survey the
principal international constraints on invisible trade, but
without the resources available to governmental enquiries the
"inventory" compiled was inevitably limited. In Appendix 1
are set out examples of constraints in the fields of insurance, banking, shipping, travel and direct investment.

These, together with portfolio investment, are briefly discussed in the remainder of the chapter.

About the examples cited in the course of the discussion a caveat needs to be entered. Government measures are always subject to change. In a period of international monetary turmoil, however, they are subject to a greater degree of change than usual. Although the specific instances cited below to illustrate points are correct at the time of writing, they may well be withdrawn or intensified or otherwise varied, which is to say they should be regarded as illustrative of a general state of affairs.

SERVICES

In keeping with the analysis thus far, the discussion of the survey focuses first on the components of invisible trade that come under the heading of services. Since the survey yielded more information on insurance, this component of invisibles is expounded on at greater length below than other components, demonstrating what should be possible in a fuller study.

Insurance Case Study

Private enterprise insurance, the only form with which this study is concerned, is a transaction between a policy-holder and an insurer whereby the former pays a premium to the latter in return for which the insurer undertakes to pay the policy-holder or some third party a sum of money, depending on the materialization of a specific risk or the occurrence of a particular event, at or during a specified time. By comparison with direct insurance, reinsurance is a transaction in which an insurer obtains from another person, the reinsurer, cover against a proportion of the risk undertaken by him in his insurance business.

The foreign insurance business of the United Kingdom is undertaken by a large number of insurance companies and Lloyd's underwriters. Lloyd's, on the one hand, is located in London and business from all over the world is brought to the underwriters through brokers. Underwriting offices are not maintained in other countries, although in some of them it is necessary for Lloyd's to become recognised insurers, under local insurance legislation, and to maintain representatives there. The insurance companies, on the other hand, in addition to their establishments in the United Kingdom, in many cases maintain a direct presence in the other countries where they operate — through a network of branches, agencies and subsidiaries which underwrite risks locally on their behalf. Thus what Lloyd's would regard as a constraint would not necessarily operate as a constraint on the insurance companies and *vice versa.*

Insurers recognise that it is one of the functions of governments to protect their citizens against loss through the operations of unscrupulous or insolvent firms. They expect, and are prepared to conform to, reasonable legislation for regulating the operations of insurers. Much depends though on the meaning of "reasonable". Whereas insurance legislation of a comprehensive nature may be accepted in a highly developed country affording prospects for the development of an insurance portfolio, and may be regarded at worst as a "constraint", legislation of a similar character in a small country affording little or no prospect of development as a field of insurance endeavour might be regarded as more in the nature of a "deterrent".

Here might be mentioned impending changes in the European Community which should effect the removal of discriminatory restrictions on insurers established in member countries and, possibly, of easing constraints on invisible earnings from them. The non-life establishment directive notified in July 1973 requires member governments to amend their insurance control legislation with a view to removing or suppressing certain provisions by February 1976. The target date may not be achieved, but member countries are not allowed, for example, to make an authorization to a Community insurer subject to the lodging of an initial deposit; it is enough that the insurer complies with the technical reserve and solvency margin provided for in the directive. Furthermore, member countries may not refuse an establishment licence to insurers from member countries, since the directive grants a right of establishment.

At present Lloyd's are not permitted an establishment in

certain countries in the European Community (Germany and Italy, for instance) and some British insurance companies have had difficulties in obtaining licences. With the introduction of legislation in line with the directive all Community insurers will have the right of establishment in other member countries. This is meant to be a first step towards a common insurance market.

In order to appreciate the constraints placed on the overseas business of British insurance companies it is interesting to note the difference between the British and typical European methods of supervision. A study on insurance in Western Europe carried out by the Organization for Economic Cooperation and Development (OECD) concluded that "as regards methods, a distinction must be made between the United Kingdom, which gives the management of an insurance concern complete liberty of action and is concerned only with the business results, and the majority of the other European market countries, whose insurance supervision laws regulate more or less precisely the conditions under which the concerns operate".[7] Indeed, when it comes to the insurance laws of the developing countries, they tend to reflect the diversity of systems in the developed world.[8]

The main constraints of a discriminatory character on the operations of insurers doing direct business in other countries are discussed below. Typical examples of those constraints are given in Appendix 1; this is not exhaustive and in some countries more than one of the constraints mentioned may apply.

No mention has been made, however, of the position of *reinsurers* whose operations tend not to be affected in the same way by the discriminatory constraints experienced by direct writing insurers. The problems of reinsurers would merit a separate study. Even so, the contribution made by reinsurance to the invisible earnings of a number of industrialized countries, particularly the United Kingdom, should not be overlooked. The point is of special relevance in the context of the present study since the obstacles in other countries to the direct writing operations of, say, British insurers can be offset to a limited extent by the acceptance of reinsurance from abroad. For example, reinsurances of nationalized concerns, and retrocessions from state re-insurance offices, may be placed in the British market.

There are numerous constraints which insurance companies face when they extend their operations to other countries. The main ones are dealt with below in the analytical framework outlined in the earlier part of this chapter.

Restriction of Foreign Competition

In certain countries, foreign insurance companies are completely, or to a large extent, excluded from doing business. Such direct action takes the form of nationalization, "domestication" or certain prohibitions on insurance abroad.

Nationalization The nationalization of an insurance industry may be achieved by

(a) an outright take-over of the private sector's portfolio by a state company or companies, or by

(b) a prohibition on all private companies from operating in the country with a monopoly of business being given to a state company.

In both cases the result is the same. The direct writing country's portfolios are seized and the flow of invisible earnings is stopped.

It is of course the prerogative of sovereign powers to conduct their domestic affairs as they see fit. But insurance is basically an international business which benefits from the widest possible spread of risks and from the widest possible access to investment opportunities. As a tertiary industry, it needs to be based on highly advanced economies and, as such, might not be deemed an appropriate activity for economies where a wide range of secondary industries have barely been established.

If developed countries are expected to concede developing countries a comparative advantage in the production of labour-intensive manufacturers, they would seem entitled, by the same token, to develop in an integrating world economy the services they are equipped to provide (among them insurance). But nationalization represents a growing threat to international transactions in private enterprise insurance.

There is a further point that ought to be made. According to international law, when an insurance industry is nationalized, compensation is payable to those whose portfolios are affected and it must be "prompt, adequate and remittable". In the experience of British insurers, however, this requirement is observed only very rarely. In Egypt when foreign business was nationalized in 1956 compensation was paid, but the amount received by foreign insurers was considered to be quite inadequate. In Ceylon, Burma and Tanzania where insurance was either nationalized outright or made the preserve of a state company no compensation has been paid.

Domestication   Another form of restriction on foreign insurance operations in some countries is a requirement that only locally-established firms may do business and, often as not, there are conditions relating to local participation in such companies. In some cases, compulsory participation, by the state or by local shareholders, is tantamount to partial nationalization, the price of such participation being unrelated to its true value. If, in order to continue operating in a country, it is decided to set up a local company in place of the existing branch or agency, money has to be made available to form the capital — causing fragmentation of free reserves. Moreover, it may be found that a company operation is not viable, having regard to the establishment and operating costs and the amount of business immediately or potentially available in the market.

In some countries, it is the insurers themselves who consider the formation of a local company a desirable and economic proposition or, alternatively, it may wish to purchase the whole or a substantial part of an established local company. But a number of countries prevent or inhibit such a course by imposing restrictions on the shareholdings which foreigners may hold in locally-constituted companies.

Certain countries require that locally-established companies must be owned and managed *entirely* by nationals. In Syria, for example, all insurance companies were required, within five years of September 1959, to be of Arab nationality; all shareholders and directors had to be Arabs.

In other countries governments have specified that companies must be *partially* owned by local shareholders. In Ghana the Insurance (Amendment) Decree of 1972 required all insurance companies to be incorporated in the country and to have at least 40 per cent of their shares in Ghanaian ownership. In Venezuela, to give another example, all insurance companies are required to have at least 50 per cent of their capital held by Venezuelans and a Venezuelan majority on their boards. Foreign participation in Spanish insurance companies is limited to 50 per cent. In Nigeria, foreign companies have to be separately incorporated in the country, and the government is gradually acquiring minority holdings in them.

In addition, the mere fulfilment, in some countries, of legal requirements does not automatically mean that a licence will be granted. Typically the supervisory authority has discretionary powers in the granting of licences. It exercises these powers mainly when economic and social conditions make it necessary to do so. Thus when it is feared that too many concerns are being established in relation to the size of the market, causing its saturation or throwing it out of "balance", the authority may either withhold further licences or apply to new applications criteria stricter than those required by existing laws in order to exclude new applicants. In a number of countries, especially in Latin America, a correlation can be shown between the relative reduction in the number of foreign concerns and the use of discretionary powers vested in supervisory authorities.[9]

Prohibitions on Insurance Abroad   In many countries there is legislation which prohibits the insuring abroad of domestic property, persons resident in the country or risks which may be incurred within the country. Examples are Argentina, Bolivia, Brazil, Colombia, Jordan, Portugal, Senegal, Uruguay and Venezuela.

Portuguese law, for instance, forbids any insurance to be taken out by, or on behalf of, any person with any concern not licensed to undertake insurance in Portugal. As a consequence, insurance may be taken out only with fully licensed Portuguese concerns or branches/agencies of foreign concerns. Where Portuguese concerns, or branches of foreign concerns, will not accept particular risks or will accept only at rates of premium deemed to be excessive, the insurance may — with the permission of the Inspectorate-General of Credit and Insurance — be placed abroad.

Whilst Swiss legislation forbids an unlicensed insurer from effecting insurances in Switzerland with residents of Switzerland it does not affect, in principle, a person's freedom to take out insurance or to choose his insurer. But a person may not take out abroad:

(a) any insurance for which a monopoly has been granted, or

(b) any compulsory insurance where the law affects the choice of insurer and requires the insurer to be licensed in Switzerland.

Throughout the federation, the Caisse Nationale Suisse d'Assurance has a monopoly of compulsory insurance against occupational injury and diseases. Seven cantons have instituted compulsory sickness insurance which has to be covered by especially constituted sickness funds, and a number have a monopoly of fire insurance covering buildings, furniture and personal effects.

In some countries, especially Latin American countries, the insurance law generally forbids insuring abroad, except in those cases which must have the approval of the insurance supervisory authority, where the local market does not have the capacity to cover risks of such size. In still other countries, although there is no formal legislation prohibiting taking insurance out abroad, there are so many bureaucratic and legal obstacles imposed that the real cost of insuring domestically is made much cheaper relative to the cost of insuring abroad. In Malaysia, the Philippines, Singapore and Vietnam it is forbidden to use the services of local agents and brokers to take out insurance with companies abroad.

Measures for Exchange Control

Apart from restrictions on remittances abroad, some countries require funds to be retained locally, partly for exchange control purposes. Some compulsory cessions to state-owned insurance companies might be thought to have been introduced in order to save foreign exchange, but it is more appropriate to discuss this practice under the heading of government discrimination.

Restrictions on Remittances   Exchange-control provisions in a number of countries cause problems for insurers with respect to the remittance of agency balances, surplus assets and reinsurance balances, although in the majority of cases it is possible eventually to obtain authorization to remit. Examples of countries where lengthy delays are often experienced are Spain, Nigeria, Kenya and the Philippines. On the other hand, there are some countries where it is extremely difficult, even impossible, to get any money out.

Localization of Funds   It is a widespread practice for governments to require the retention of substantial funds locally. The stated purposes are:

   (a) to provide security for policy-holders;
   (b) to provide much needed investment capital for local industry; and
   (c) to reduce the export of foreign exchange.

The very nature of general insurance business means that firms must hold fairly liquid reserves to meet possible contingencies. Most countries which have established legislation covering solvency requirements have laid down formulae as to the way in which solvency should be calculated. The law may for instance require that life assurance companies use specific technical factors in calculating the actuarial value of their reserves – such as particular mortality tables or particular interest rates.

Requirements for the localization of funds may relate to solvency margins, to guarantee deposits or to technical reserves. Insurers, however, prefer the utmost freedom in the field of investment so that maximum advantage can be taken of securities suitable for their purpose wherever they can be found, their world-wide funds being available to meet their commitments in all countries where they operate. In recent years, though, insurance companies – at least in the United Kingdom – have been taking the view that technical reserve requirements of the above type are acceptable, *provided* domestic and foreign companies are treated similarly and investment opportunities are available in the country giving (i) security, (ii) liquidity, particularly for short-term business, and (iii) adequate yield. But these criteria are not met in many of the countries in which such provisions apply.

There is an exception to this general view. In the fields of marine and aviation insurance the localization of technical reserves should not be required. For in those fields, reserves for outstanding claims must be freely available so that funds can be immediately sent, without any restrictions, to where they are required. Claims in these fields may not − indeed probably will not − arise in the territory in which the business has been written.

Government Discrimination

Very often efforts to discriminate in favour of domestic insurers, sometimes wholly or partly state-owned, and against foreign insurers are broached by direct means.

Compulsory Cessions In an increasing number of countries state-owned insurance companies have been established and all other companies operating in that particular market are required to cede to it a part of the risks they write there.

There can be no objection to a state-owned company transacting reinsurance in competition with the existing reinsurance market. If the terms were attractive the private-enterprise companies might well wish to avail themselves of the state-owned company's services for some of their reinsurance needs. But the introduction of compulsory cessions distorts the proper function of reinsurance. It takes from the private-enterprise companies, business which they could handle without reinsurance assistance; in fact, many insurers do not require such assistance, except with a few of their largest insurances. For liability insurances, what the insurer requires is reinsurance protection at a modest cost against the occasional large claim which may arise under even the smallest policy; it does not require an automatic reinsurance participation in every claim.

Inasmuch as compulsory cessions do little to meet the reinsurance needs of the private-enterprise companies, their only purpose would appear to be to secure for a state-owned company a share in the existing market. There is no reason why governments should not enter the insurance business in the hope of deriving some profit. But it does not appear in the best interest of the market for them to employ compulsion. Compulsory reinsurance is no substitute for much of the reinsurance normally effected by private-enterprise companies; it might be deemed to be, in effect, an expropriation of a part of their business.

Furthermore, compulsory cessions can lead to heavy accumulations of state-owned companies, calling for unusually heavy retrocessions abroad. Where a particularly large insurance is concerned the risk is rapidly spread around the market by coinsurance and reinsurance facilities. But, however much the market may seek to spread the load in this way, the state-owned company would, because of the compulsion, find itself burdened with a disproportionate share of the total value insured. In respect of liability risks to third parties, too, the assumption of a fixed share of even the smallest policy would expose the state-owned company to quite heavy losses.

It may be thought that if the private-enterprise companies were compelled to cede reinsurance to a state-owned company they would place rather less reinsurance in other countries and the country in question would benefit from a saving in foreign exchange. As has been explained already, however, compulsory cessions may do little to reduce a private-enterprise company's need for reinsurance protection and, in fact, a new demand for foreign exchange would be created by the state-owned company's own reinsurance arrangements in respect of business ceded to it.

Public Procurement   Discrimination is practised in some countries in favour of domestic insurance companies and against foreign ones by governments bringing pressure to bear on public enterprises and private concerns which depend on government patronage to deal with local companies. To illustrate, in Argentina any firm or individual who enjoys any of a wide variety of vaguely defined concessions, franchises, tax abatements and so on must insure their interests exclusively with Argentine insurance companies. All government, provincial, municipal and other official insurance interests must be placed with Argentine companies. Similarly, only Argentine companies may insure imports into Argentina which are for the account of the importer, and commission paid to foreign companies on the first 30 per cent of the compulsory cessions to the State Reinsurance Entity is restricted to the original acquisition commission cost without any reimbursement of other acquisition costs, whereas domestic companies receive a much higher rate of commission.

By way of further illustration, all government insurance in Kenya, including statutory boards, local authorities and cooperatives, are directed to the Kenya National Assurance Company. In Queensland, in Australia, the State Government Insurance Company have a monopoly of Workmen's Compensation Insurance. In certain parts of Switzerland, fire insurance on buildings is compulsory, and has to be placed with the cantonal insurance companies.

Employment of Expatriates

Where companies are doing business abroad through branches, or head office-controlled subsidiaries, it has been customary for the more senior positions to be staffed by expatriates. This has partly been for the purpose of having company policy carried out by staff familiar with the traditions and philosophy of the company and partly, too, because of a lack of qualified local recruits, particularly in the developing countries.

National aspirations have dictated increasingly that both the management and senior positions should be localized. Insurers have recognized these aspirations and are training a growing number of local recruits to the highest level which continually improving educational standards will allow. But the policy followed by some developing countries of imposing excessive restrictions on the issue of work permits for key expatriate personnel militates against the efficiency of local managements and the training of local personnel.

Conflicts in UNCTAD

From the outset, the United Nations Conference on Trade and Development (UNCTAD) has interested itself in insurance and reinsurance, recommending at its first session in Geneva in 1964 that the developed countries should cooperate in helping less developed countries to strengthen their national insurance and reinsurance markets and support "all reasonable measures" to that end.[10] Over the years UNCTAD has conducted several studies and prepared more detailed recommendations which were considered at the third session held in Santiago in 1972.[11]

In the nature of things, recommendations of United Nations meetings are difficult to summarize, given the extent to which they are hedged with qualifications. It is unfortunate though that UNCTAD recommendations on insurance and reinsurance do not recognize the case for greater freedom from constraints which has been advanced by a number of developed countries and, indeed, support some of the adverse factors listed above.

Banking

Controls on banking and especially foreign banks are in many ways comparable with controls on insurance concerns. (See Appendix 1, pages 113-21.) In most countries there are controls on the establishment of new branches, on capital requirements, on the allocation of their portfolio of assets, on the maximum interest rates payable on the various types of deposit liabilities, on the extent to which profits may be repatriated and on the employment of nationals. One of the interesting features of these controls, and especially those that discriminate against foreign banks, is that their necessity is frequently justified on the ground that such control is an integral part of monetary policy in general.

In some countries the establishment of foreign banks is forbidden by law. This is not only true of developing countries like Algeria, Turkey and Tanzania. It is also true of developed countries such as Australia and Canada. (See the section in Appendix 1 on banking.) In other countries, foreign banks *per se* are also forbidden, but banks can be set up with varying maximum proportions of foreign ownership which result in a minority foreign interest, such as in Mexico and Venezuela. In other countries foreign banks can be established (in principle), subject to a licence being granted by the relevant licensing authority, but in practice such a licence may prove extremely difficult to obtain. Brazil, for instance, has not issued such a licence since the early 1960s.

As with insurance, prudent banking requires that banks hold liquid assets, in this case as a reserve against deposit withdrawals. To ensure the solvency of the banking system, and in particular to protect depositors, most countries' monetary authorities impose minimum ratio(s) of specified reserve assets to various categories of deposit or total liabilities. In addition the monetary authorities may direct the extent to which the remainder of bank assets can be held in certain types of assets, maybe ensuring that a minimum proportion of non-liquid assets are invested in government securities or that a certain proportion of loans are granted to certain sectors of the economy. While there may not be specific discrimination against foreign banks *vis-à-vis* domestic banks in applying the rules, the very fact that bank behaviour is different because the existence of these rules will affect the banks' profitability and in turn the scale of their operations. Another form of control is the fixing either of the level of interest rates or of ceilings to their levels, both those paid on deposits and charged on advances.

One of the constraints faced by foreign banks, especially in developing countries, is the demand that they employ a certain percentage of nationals on their staff.

Shipping

Civil aviation and shipping constitute the two main areas of transport. The numerous forms of discrimination against foreign shipping are discussed below under flag discrimination, cabotage laws and operating subsidies.

Flag Discrimination

Flag discrimination is an extremely difficult term to define. The International Chamber of Commerce refers to it as "a general rather than exact term, comprising a wide variety of acts and pressures exerted by governments in order to direct cargoes to national flag ships, regardless of the commercial considerations which would otherwise apply to the routeing of the cargo".[12] In the United Kingdom, the Rochdale Committee of Inquiry into Shipping stated, in a similar vein, that "there is no precise definition of the term 'flag discrimination'. It embraces a wide variety of measures and pressures exerted by governments, which are designed to direct trade to ships of their national flag."[13] Discrimination may take several forms. (i) It may be a unilateral action of a government discriminating against ships of all other flags. (ii) It may be a bilateral agreement between two countries discriminating in favour of ships of their own flags and against those of all other countries. (iii) Or it may be a group of countries discriminating against ships of all other flags except their own.

Discrimination itself may take any one of several forms as set out below:

(a) A law, regulation or some other administrative measure, including informal measures, may stipulate that a certain percentage of all or certain types of cargoes (such as government-owned or sponsored cargo) is to be reserved to national flag ships.

(b) Preferential rates of customs and/or other dues may be applied.

(c) National ships may be reserved for imports and exports qualifying for preferential credit facilities, preferential rates of tax and special tariff concessions.

(d) Import and export licensing and exchange controls (for example, blocking foreign currency earned by foreign ships, converting it at an unfavourable rate, compelling foreign lines to accept freight payments in inconvertible local currencies) may be used together with the terms of shipment — that is, buying free on board (f.o.b.) and selling at prices that include cost, insurance and freight (c.i.f.) to direct cargoes to national flag ships.

(e) Discriminatory pricing may be applied with

respect to harbour, light pilotage and tonnage dues, consular fees, taxes on freight revenue and so on.

Cabotage Laws

Laws reserving either a proportion *or* all of a country's coastal trade to national flag ships are widespread. For many countries the extent of its coastline means that the total amount of trade reserved in this way is very small. But for some countries such as India, Brazil, Chile and the United States goods are transported across large distances in open water. The United States reserves to national flag ships the coastal trade between the East and West coasts via the Panama canal and also to and from Alaska, Honolulu and the United States islands in the Caribbean. Among the countries of Western Europe, only Belgium, Britain, Denmark, the Netherlands and Norway do not protect their coastal trade.

The one exception to this picture of general restriction is the transport of oil and oil products which is carried in tankers of ocean-going capability by the large international oil companies. The Rochdale Report, in commenting on this, argued: "The major oil companies can achieve economies in operation by deploying the tanker fleets under their control on a world scale; many countries have recognized the value of this and have applied their coastal trade restrictions in a flexible manner. As a result, so long as their national flag vessels are employed by the international oil companies to an agreed extent within their total shipping operations these companies may not be required to use vessels of the national flag for all the relevant coastal shipments which they make."[14]

Operating Subsidies

Subsidies are paid by various governments to shipping operators. They come in a variety of forms and have been classified by UNCTAD in nine different categories:[15]

    (a) Direct subsidies for the construction, purchase and improvement of ships;

    (b) Scrap-and-build schemes;

(c) Loans at low rates of interest;

(d) Accelerated depreciation provisions on investment allowances or grants;

(e) Exemption from income tax and other tax privileges;

(f) Reimbursement of harbour dues, pilotage expenses, canal dues, etc. paid overseas or in home ports;

(g) Losses of state-owned fleets or shipyards borne by general taxation;

(h) Contracts for the carriage of mail on favourable terms; and

(i) Payment of freight at rates above world charter rates for government cargoes carried in national flag ships.

An example of general subsidies are those given in Italy, France and Spain.

For many years the United States Administration has paid a subsidy to shipowners which provide passenger and cargo liner services on routes which are regarded as essential to the national interest. The stipulation is simply that the ships must have been built in the United States and their crews must be American citizens. Under the Maritime Act of October 1970, direct operating subsidies are extended to bulk carriers and the basis of the amount of the subsidy has been changed from what it was previous to this act, so that it is linked to the difference between wage costs in the United States and elsewhere. Under the Act there is also an extension for the eligibility for tax deferment privileges to all American operations in the foreign trade of the United States.

Travel

Foreign currency is earned by foreigners visiting and spending money in a country. The only real restriction which could be thought of as a constraint in this field is the imposition by governments of restrictions on the amount of currency their residents may take out of the country.[16] Such restrictions are imposed from time to time. Indeed, at the time of writing, France imposes a limit of 1,500 francs per person which may be taken out twice a year for tourist travel to foreign countries; Greece, a limit of 200 drachmas for one trip per year; South Africa, a limit of 2,000 rands per adult for tourist travel in a calendar year; and Ghana, which is very restrictive, a limit of 55 new cedis annual travel allowance. Typically the imposition of such a requirement as this is used as a method of reducing the size of the balance-of-payments deficit.

MONETARY MOVEMENTS

Direct Investment

There are a variety of controls in existence which attempt to regulate not only the inflows of direct foreign investment to particular countries — something which is particularly relevant to British direct investment abroad and in turn to British invisible earnings — but also attempt to regulate outflows of direct foreign investment, especially from certain highly industrialized countries to others.

There are four forms of constraints. First, there is the exclusion of direct foreign investments from certain industries in particular countries on the grounds of national defence, security and so forth. For example, direct foreign investment in the United States is prohibited in fresh water shipping, domestic radio communication and domestic air transport. In Mexico, direct foreign investment other than by private individuals is prohibited in banking and insurance. Ghana excludes foreign capital from certain retail, wholesale and transportation operations.

Secondly, some countries have a requirement, constituting a constraint, that foreign ownership in either certain or all industries must not rise above a certain percentage of the total equity interest of the particular company. In Japan foreign direct investment in those industries listed in Category A of the Liberalization List (447 industries) will only obtain automatic approval if the foreign capital ratio does not exceed 50 per cent. Over recent years this list has been increasingly liberalized. In Tanzania large investments usually require majority participation by Tanzanian capital.

Government policies which set down "guidelines" that restrict, to a greater or lesser extent, the activities of foreign companies are a third form of constraint. In Australia companies with more than 25 per cent equity interest are allowed reasonably free access to the Australian capital market for raising short-term working capital, but the granting of access to the long-term capital market depends on such factors as the amount of overseas funds invested in the company and the percentage of the equity in the company which is held by Australians. In Ghana foreign-controlled companies which raise capital locally are not permitted to transfer either profits or dividends abroad.

Finally, although not a direct constraint on a country's invisible exports, voluntary guidelines on the outflow of direct investment capital (especially in developed countries), comparable with Britain's exchange-control criteria, were important in the 1960s. In the United States annual limits were placed on net direct capital outflow plus reinvested earnings, restricting the total amount of investment each year to a percentage of the amount invested in the base period, as well as limiting the total amount of short-term financial assets which can be held abroad by direct investors. Investors could either choose a global maximum of $2m per year with which to undertake foreign direct investment or else they could accept the three regional ceilings which were placed on investment: one region being the less developed countries, another being countries which were thought to depend on a substantial inflow of capital which could not be adequately met from non-American sources, the third being the rest of the world. This last group of countries, to which there was a virtual embargo on net capital flows, included most of Western Europe, although not the United Kingdom. The measures were removed in the early 1970s, but they represent a significant constraint of a kind that could easily recur − perhaps as a consequence of "oil payments" problems.

Portfolio Investment

There are two main types of obstacles to the movements of portfolio investment between, for illustrative purposes,

Britain and other countries apart from the foreign exchange control restrictions.[17] First, there are various actions taken by foreign governments to improve their net balance-of-payments position, by restricting either the outflow or the inflow of portfolio capital. Among developed countries the United States, since the early 1960s, has had a policy to restrict the outflow of portfolio investment from the United States. In 1963 the United States Administration imposed an interest-equalization tax on American residents who purchased foreign stocks and debt obligations from foreigners. The tax is at present 0.75 per cent, but there are certain major exemptions; investments in less developed countries, purchases from other American holders, foreign debt which was acquired in connection with United States exports, if the tax imperils the stability of the international monetary system such as Canadian debt issues, and bank loans denominated either in American dollars or foreign currencies that are made by foreign branches of United States banks to foreigners. In addition to the interest-equalization tax, the Federal Reserve Board supervises a voluntary foreign credit restraint programme, which lays down guidelines for bank and non-bank financial intermediaries with respect to their foreign assets.

France maintains special controls over borrowing abroad and although various loans are exempt from the need for prior authorization (borrowing by industrial firms for work abroad, borrowing to finance trade, loans related to international merchanting transactions, and so on), borrowing in the Euro-franc market has been severely restricted. In many if not most developing countries there are extremely stringent regulations on foreign portfolio investment.

Numerous countries — France perhaps most notably — impose restrictions on the issue of foreign securities on their stock exchanges. In Italy only international financial institutions such as the IBIO and the BEI have been allowed to issue shares. Foreign issues require approval in Holland, which is not normally given, except for international institutions or countries to which the Netherlands is under special obligation, such as former colonies. In Sweden non-residents cannot issue and place securities on the Swedish capital market.

But secondly, and quite apart from countries' actions to improve their balance of payments in a general sense there are various administrative, legal and fiscal barriers which are the result of particular countries' historical development and which, while not necessarily and certainly not explicitly used as instruments to influence the balance of payments, impede the free flow of capital between countries. Under this section would be included such factors as different tax systems, differential rates of stamp duty on domestic and foreign new issues, the variety of standards with respect to the amount of information which companies have to disclose in their accounts, the procedure for transferring registered stocks, and differences in stock exchange dealing techniques and practices, in settlement procedures, and in quotation rules.[18]

NOTES

1. The OECD has maintained a long-standing interest in restrictive business practices. See, for example, *Guide to Legislation on Restrictive Business Practices* (Paris: OECD Secretariat, 1962), a loose-leaf publication in six volumes with supplements. Also see other OECD publications: *Glossary of Terms relating to Restrictive Business Practices* (1965); *Refusal to Sell,* Report of the Committee of Experts on Restrictive Business Practices (1969); and *Market Power and the Law* (1970), a study of restrictive practice laws of OECD countries and, too, of the European Community dealing with market power.

   In respect of the European Community, see *The Problem of Concentration in the Common Market* (Brussels: Commission of the European Community, 1966); and *The First Report on Competition Policy* (1972) and the second report (1973) of the Commission. For a discussion of competition policy in the European Community in a broader economic context, see Bela Balassa, "Industrial Policy in the European Common Market", *Banca Nazionale del Lavaro Quarterly Review,* Rome, December 1973.

   As for the approach of the European Free Trade Association, see Adrienne Szokoloczy-Syllaba, *EFTA: Restrictive Business Practices* (Bern: Verlag Stampfli, 1973).

   For a description of the liner conference system in shipping, see the Rochdale Report, *op. cit.,* pp. 116-36.

2. A good analysis of the way in which restrictions on portfolio capital movements are tied up with individual countries' balance-of-payments adjustment policies is given in Cooper, *The Economics of Interdependence* (New York: McGraw-Hill, for the Council on Foreign Relations, 1963).

3. For a more general analysis of the economic effects of government procurement policy, see Brian Hindley, *Britain's Position on Non-tariff Protection*, Thames Essays No. 4 (London: Trade Policy Research Centre, 1972).

4. The most comprehensive accounts of foreign exchange controls can be found in successive issues of the *Annual Report on Exchange Restrictions* (Washington: International Monetary Fund).

5. For an extensive analytical treatment of the subject, see: Milton Friedman, "Controls on Interest Rates Paid by Banks", *Journal of Money, Credit and Banking*, Columbus, February 1970; and Albert M. Cox, "Regulation of Interest on Bank Deposits", *Michigan Business Studies*, Ann Arbor, Vol. 17, No. 14, 1966.

6. Further details of the German controls can be found in *Report of the Deutsche Bundesbank for 1971*, Frankfurt, 1971.

7. *Supervision of Private Insurance in Europe*, No. 15/283 (Paris: OECD Secretariat, 1963), para. 264, p. 37.

8. Although insurance legislation in what were formerly colonies was sometimes based on that of the metropolitan power, it was by no means the universal practice; and this past association cannot be taken as a guide to the present position.

9 *Study on Insurance Legislation and Supervision in Developing Countries, op. cit.*

10. *Ibid.*, TD/B/C.3/29 and TD/B/C.3/AC.2/1, Annex 1, p. 1, for these UNCTAD recommendations.

11. See the resultion, and preamble, agreed at the third UNCTAD on 6 May 1972 by the Group of 77 and Group B Countries (except the United Kingdom which reserved its position). The resolution was reported in the *Policy Holder Insurance Journal*, London, 2 June 1972.

12. "Flag Discrimination", *Transport and Communications*, M. K. Document No. 321/162 (Paris: International Chamber of Commerce, 1969).

13. Rochdale Report, *op. cit.*, para. 147.

14. *Ibid.*, para. 145.

15. *Development of Expansion of Merchant Marines in Developing Countries: The Nature and Extent of Cargo Reservation*, TD/B/C.4/63. (Geneva: UNCTAD, 1970), p. 6.

16. A comprehensive account of the problems associated with travel in OECD countries is to be found in *International Tourism and Tourism Policy in OECD Member Countries* (Paris: OECD Secretariat, 1971).

17. See, in particular, the *Twenty Second Annual Report on Exchange Restrictions, op. cit.;* "A Short History of UK Foreign Exchange Control", *Bank of England Quarterly Bulletin*, London, September 1967; Exchange Control Act 1947 and *Notices to Authorized Depositories* arising out of the Act; and *Capital Markets in Europe*, a report of the Economic Research Group of the Amsterdam-Rotterdam Bank, Deutsche Bank, Midland Bank, Société Générale de Bank and General Bank Maatschappij.

18. See in particular *Capital Markets in Atlantic Economic Relationships* (Paris: Atlantic Institute, 1967); *Development of Capital Markets* (London: International Federation of Stock Exchanges, 1969); and *Admission of Securities to Official Quotation* (London: International Federation of Stock Exchanges, 1971).

Also see *Barriers to Issuing and Trading of Foreign Bonds and Shares on the National Capital Markets of Certain OECD Countries* (Paris: OECD Secretariat for the Business and Industry Advisory Committee, 1969): *The Development of a European Capital Market* (Brussels: EEC Commission, 1966).

In addition, see *The Capital Market, International Capital Movements and Restrictions on Capital Operations: Germany,* (Paris, OECD Secretariat, 1969) and subsequent country studies on Austria (1970), Denmark (1970), Norway (1970), Spain (1971) and Switzerland (1972); besides E. B. Northcliffe, *Taxes on the Issue and Negotiation of Securities* (Paris: OECD Secretariat, 1970).

CHAPTER 3

Defence of the Barriers to Invisible Trade

The effects of constraints on invisible trade can only be considered by comparison with a theoretical world in which there is complete freedom of trade in invisibles. Under such an assumption, each country would produce those services in which it had a comparative advantage over the rest of the world, meaning that the total output of shipping, banking and insurance services in the world as a whole would be produced at the least possible cost. Given the world prices of providing invisible services, the United Kingdom would be induced to supply a certain amount of those services which it found profitable to provide at those particular prices. The ratio of invisible to visible trade for Britain would be at an optimal level reflecting in turn British cost advantage over the rest of the world in the production of services by comparison with the production of visible goods. Such a statistic would not only show the comparative advantage over other countries in the provision of invisible services. It would also mean that the real income of Britain was at a higher level than it would be for any other proportion of invisible to visible trade.

In such a world, and subject to appropriate exchange-rate adjustment by the United Kingdom to maintain an overall balance of external payments, no artificial controls would be imposed on the movement of capital — either on inflows or outflows of portfolio capital or direct investment. Direct investment would take place from the United Kingdom by those firms which were able to earn abroad a higher return on capital; investment would take place in the United Kingdom by those foreign concerns which were able to earn a higher rate of return on their capital in Britain than in their own countries. The position with respect to portfolio investment would be comparable. Funds would move to those countries which offered the highest rate of return, when the rate of return was calculated to include the effects of possible exchange-rate changes, as well as the cost of insuring against such changes. That world would be incompatible with the present international monetary system unless each country were to pursue similar monetary policies. If countries refused to harmonize their domestic economic policies then only the flexibility of their exchange rates would ensure that they were insulated from differing economic policies being pursued by the rest of the world.

Various arguments have been used by countries and industries to defend the imposition of barriers to trade in the field of invisibles: the need to protect an infant industry against foreign competition, the necessity for certain in-dustries to be maintained under domestic control, the need for a means of retaliation by developing countries against the discriminatory practices of developed countries, and the need for the balance of payments to move from deficit to surplus. In most cases the arguments for restricting trade in the field of "invisibles" are the same as those for restricting trade in the field of visibles.

Before going into these arguments (which are bound to be discussed more widely as the constraints on invisible earnings become a more serious focus of inter-governmental attention) it is clear that a greater understanding is required of the specific problems encountered in particular fields of activity between specific countries. Such has been found to be the case in respect of non-tariff distortions of international trade in merchandise. What is required is considerably more economic research on industrial organization and on specific problems in the conduct of international business. Here there is a point that might be reiterated, having been made elsewhere by Harry G. Johnson, of the University of Chicago, whose contribution to the study of international economics, at a practical as well as a theoretical level, has been formidable.

For economic research on industrial organization and on international trade, whether visible or invisible, suffers from a disadvantage not encountered, or encountered only to a far lesser extent, in other fields. The disadvantage, briefly stated, is that businessmen are accustomed to think of research on industry and trade as a way of helping them make money, not as a way of enabling the rest of society to understand them and their problems.

"In the context of policy research, this usually means that businessmen are happy with and pleased by research that finds the mote in their neighbour's eye, but distressed and even angry with research that finds the beam in their own. More concretely," Professor Johnson continues, "they are delighted with any disclosure of discriminatory trade practices pursued by other firms and governments, but they are upset by any disclosure of similar practices on their own parts which they would like to have regarded as entirely warranted defensive measures against foreign unfairness. This attitude makes it extremely difficult for self-styled 'practical men' to accept the results of practical research that regards them, not as heroes fighting a war against insuperable odds, and deserving only of praise for their valour, but as specimens of the genus *homo sapiens* reacting in economically predictable ways to the economic environment that nature and their fellow men have established for them.

"Research on industry and trade is likely to be a poor relation of economic research in general so long as 'practical men' insist on judging it by the question: 'What does it do for me?' Instead it should be judged by the question: 'What does it do for the country?' The question that economic research into monopolistic and other restrictive practices should raise in the mind of the practical businessman is not: 'Am I really a bad man?' To that question the answer cannot be 'yes', because he knows that he is loyal to his company and good to his wife and children. Rather the question should be: 'If other people in society consider me to be a bad man, why is it that I am constrained to behave that way in order to survive?' The answer frequently is that his fellow men, through the political process, have constrained him to behave in one way, but insist on judging him as if he were free to behave, and should behave, in another."[1]

Until this is properly recognized it is not likely that much further progress can be made in the liberalization of international commerce. Appropriate provisions need to be made to help industries adjust to changes in their economic environment as a result of either domestic developments or international competition. That is the direction in which economic policy discussion has been moving on interventions in visible trade now that tariffs have been reduced to very low levels. In other words, the rationale of domestic policies relating to industrial organization and regional balance *et cetera* is being questioned far more. In due course the policies of governments towards services can be expected to be subjected to closer scrutiny for similar reasons — to do with the growing integration, and increasing interdependence, of the world economy. And so what of the justifications for constraints on invisible earnings?

Infant Industry Argument

The infant-industry argument has a long and distinguished history as a rationalization for public assistance to new industries. It is particularly used by various developing countries as a justification for state aid to the development of national merchant shipping fleets, insurance business and banking.[2] A report prepared by the UNCTAD Secretariat on the *Establishment or Expansion of Merchant Marines in Developing Countries* states that "the infant industry argument for assistance to liner shipping in developing countries is a relevant one because of (i) the high capital costs in setting up the industry which would mean that it would have to start on a small scale, (ii) the significant economies of scale (particularly know-how and labour and management costs) which can reasonably be expected to be reaped in course of time and (iii) the advantages in the form of trade connections and customer goodwill which established owners enjoy and which will take a new owner some time to acquire during which he will be at a disadvantage". In considering whether the method of assistance given should be subsidy or some form of preference, the report concludes that "on the whole subsidies are probably a better form of assistance than preferences".[3] But it argues that "there is also the fact that by allowing the national lines to secure more cargo than they otherwise would, discrimination may make it possible for them to reap the economies of scale which are particularly relevant to the liner business".[4]

The infant-industry argument is an attempt to rationalize temporary government assistance to an industry, even within an economy which operates on a *laissez-faire* basis. It is an assertion that over a restricted period of time, temporary assistance can be justified for an industry which is being newly developed because, although the short-run costs of production are high relative to the long-run costs of production (as reflected by the prices of foreign producers), there can nevertheless be in due course an expansion in the output of the industry which could become viable in the international market in competition with foreign firms. The argument is quite different from the argument of external economies. External diseconomies or economies are something permanent, reflecting the state of technology, which is slow to change. Because of their permanence they require constant government intervention in order to remove the distortion.

The attempt, however, to claim the applicability of the infant-industry case to a particular industry, in order to justify protection, is neither a necessary nor a sufficient condition for specific assistance. If a correct investment appraisal is carried out, the high initial per-unit costs of setting up a new industry will be set against the reduced future per-unit costs. And if the net rate of return on the investment exceeds the net rate of return on the highest yielding alternative investment, the industry should be set up. Indeed, if an efficient private capital market exists, such an industry will in fact be established.

The fact of infancy is therefore not an argument for protection. In his article on optimal trade intervention and domestic distortion, Professor Johnson states that "to provide an argument for government intervention, it must be demonstrated either that the social rate of return necessary to induce the investment exceeds the private rate of return on the investment, or that the private rate of return necessary to induce the investment exceeds the private and social rates of return on alternative investment by a wide enough margin to make a socially profitable investment privately unprofit-able".[5] Examples of justifiable reasons for intervention are (i) the social benefits of learning a particular production technique in, say, shipping or insurance, (ii) unwillingness by entrepreneurs to take risks and (iii) imperfections in the capital market. Even when these factors are taken into account, however, it is in general more efficient to subsidize rather than protect the infant industries. All too often developing countries claim the applicability of the infant-industry argument for protection without really applying it properly.

Domestic Ownership of Key Industries

An argument which on the face of it seems impregnable is that it is essential that, in the national interests, certain industries should both be owned and controlled by citizens of the country. This is one of the arguments used by a number of countries to defend their cabotage laws restricting coastal trade to ships of their own flag, by many others to exclude foreign airlines, by still others to exclude direct foreign investment and by other countries to nationalize insurance.

In the United States the Jones Act, which restricts coastal trade to ships of the American flag, is said to be a measure to further the national security of the country. A defence of the Jones Act argues that "foreign-flag ships in the US domestic trade could be withdrawn from that trade and potentially used against us in a war at sea".[6] Defenders of the Act also quote with favour a report in 1963 to the Senate Commerce Committee, by Vice Admiral John Sylvester, that "the ability of the domestic deep-water fleet to provide essentially coastal and inter-coastal movements of priority material might well be crucial. Of course *to be available for immediate use these ships must be active and operating commercially at the time they are first needed.*"[7]

There are two interesting sides to this argument. In the first place, little attempt is made to estimate the likely need to use these ships in case of an emergency, or to consider what alternative ways there might be found of achieving a similar objective through the use of road and rail. Secondly, no attempt is made to compute the cost of running ships which are at present inefficient on the grounds that some time in the future they may become extremely useful; and therefore, because of the increase in demand, the price which they would be able to charge for their services would be greater or equal to the marginal cost of using them.

In certain cases the reason for state control and national-ization has been ideological. It is claimed, however, that in the majority of developing countries public ownership is the only way of obtaining national control of an industry, due mainly to the fact that there is not sufficient national entrepreneurial ability for the industry to be run privately. W. R. Malinowski, as Director of the Division for Invisibles in the UNCTAD Secretariat, has argued that in the case of insurance in a large number of instances developing countries have come to the conclusion that dependence on unsound domestic private enterprises and uncontrolled private foreign companies can prejudice the achievement of their economic objectives. Uninhibited competition among large numbers of foreign and domestic companies, in what are in most cases very small markets, leads to waste and the insufficient balance of risks. He goes on to suggest that "perhaps a few enterprises by issuing a large number of risks can provide a less costly and sounder insurance service".[8] (Many inter-national insurers would contest this view, pointing to the examples of several developing countries where a state mono-poly of insurance, far from producing these benefits, has led to rigidity and stagnation of the market.) Other motives for the domestic ownership of insurance companies are the role of life assurance in contributing to domestic savings, which can be channelled into investment to produce a higher rate of economic growth, and the savings which might be achieved in the balance of payments.

Foreign Banks and Monetary Policy

Another variation of argument used to justify the exclusion of foreign-owned enterprises, particularly banks, is that domestic ownership is essential if a country is to be able to conduct its own economic policy. Because the control of banking is crucial to the conduct of monetary policy, it is essential that banks be owned by domestic citizens, who are subject to domestic law.

Therefore the 1967 Bank Act in Canada limits the ownership by foreign residents of the voting shares of a Canadian bank to 25 per cent of the total ownership and makes particular provisions for the Mercantile Bank (owned by First National City Bank of New York) to meet these requirements over a certain period. In the case of Canada the problem seems to have been that in the past various foreign-owned financial institutions would only agree to accept the technique of "moral suasion", as used by the Bank of Canada, if it was to be made law. If it was not law they felt free to carry on and arrange their affairs to their advantage — although within the existing legal framework.

In Canada the Royal Commission on Banking and Finance examined, in 1965, the question of foreign banking and recommended that "a high degree of Canadian ownership of financial institutions is in itself healthy and desirable and that the balance of advantage is against foreign control of Canadian banks", although they also recommended that foreign banks be able to apply for the right to open agencies which would be able to conduct all aspects of banking business except the taking of deposit liabilities in Canada.

The report put forward two major arguments to justify the exclusion of foreign-owned banks. First, there was the possibility that foreign-owned banks, and especially American-owned banks, could acquire ownership in Canadian financial institutions "in order to promote their own business interests in Canada".[9] In particular, they might be in a position to obtain the business of corporations whose parent companies already dealt with the parent bank, "without offering better or cheaper service in our banking market". Secondly, foreign banks "might be less sympathetic, than those controlled in Canada, to the wishes and policies of the Canadian monetary authorities".[10]

With respect to the first of these arguments, the report itself recognized that the extent to which business would be reallocated from domestic to foreign-owned banks for non-

economic reasons was likely to be very small, for corporations typically dealt with a number of banks and could
therefore resist pressures which were against their own
interests. The report recognized, too, that "the Canadian
banks, being large themselves, would undoubtedly resist such
a tendency".[11] In connection with the second argument
above, the Commission acknowledged that foreign-owned
banks would "be subject to the same regulation and control
as those owned in Canada and would be affected in the same
way by policy action".[12] They were also careful to point out
that foreign banks would not have easier access to foreign
funds in periods of tight money than the Canadian-owned
banks which have extensive operations in foreign markets.
Something which the report did not point out, but which is
important, is that to the extent a competitive banking system
develops in Canada following the changes introduced in the
1967 Bank Act it is increasingly difficult for the Bank of
Canada to conduct monetary policy through the use of moral
suasion even if the banks are domestically owned.

When these various qualifications are taken into account,
the exclusion of foreign banks amounts to no more than a
straight concession to the demands of Canadian nationalists
so that their own industry should be protected, at least on
the domestic side, not only from supposed American
domination but also from American competition. If the Bank
of Canada wishes to issue orders to the chartered banks, or
any other financial institutions, on such matters as the
composition of bank lending or the maximum rates payable
on time deposits, it should ensure that the federal laws
applicable to banking contain adequate provisions for control
of foreign owned as well as domestic banks.

Retaliation against the Constraints of Other Countries

The need to be able to retaliate against the measures of other
countries is an argument frequently used in the field of
shipping to justify the system of preferences which various
underdeveloped countries have instituted in order to ensure a
certain amount of business for ships of their own flag.

The basis of the argument is that liner conferences are restrictive and use their control of various routes to their own advantage. It is further argued that they have either entirely excluded foreign competition from their particular route or else, having admitted new members, allowed them only a trifling proportion of business. Countries wishing to develop their own shipping lines can only counter this particular restrictive practice by another — namely, flag discrimination. The fact that the major part of world trade is carried in ships of developed countries is well documented. In 1970, for example, 62.4 per cent of the volume of all exports, and 16.5 per cent of the volume of all imports, were generated by the developing countries. In spite of this, developing countries controlled only 7.4 per cent of world gross tonnage in shipping.

The conclusion of the UNCTAD report on the establishment of merchant marines in developing countries argues that although subsidies are probably a better form of assistance than preferences, "it is also true that a government can more easily support shipping by means of preferential arrangements covering national cargoes, and the temptation to give a national line a good start by ensuring its access to cargo is often strong. This is particularly so if a national line has been refused entry to the relevant conference, or if in the conference it cannot obtain a fair share of the cargo."[13] And it then goes on to quote in a footnote an example taken from S. G. Sturmey's *British Shipping and World Competition* where he argued that "Brazil has adopted both the bilateral treaty and an over-all rule that 70 per cent of Brazilian imports must travel in Brazilian ships. It should be noted, however, that this 70 per cent rule was adopted, in part at least, in retaliation to the action of the conference covering the deferred rebate system and so shut the non-conference ships of Lloyd Brasiliero from the trade."[14]

The criticism of the existing system is then that in general the type of competition which has been encouraged by the conference system provides a service of "higher quality, higher speed and therefore higher cost service than most shippers require"[15] and that, in particular, it discriminates against potential new entrants. Because of the price fixing in the conference system, competition centres mainly on the quality of the service, so that shippers have only a limited opportunity of being able to choose between different types of services at different prices.

Against this, it is argued that conference lines compete against tramp owners for bulk cargoes, against airlines for break-bulk cargoes and against outsider lines for all types of cargoes. Some conferences are even competing against road and rail land-bridges. To the extent that there are alternative sources of supply it might be added that most conferences are competing with each other. The competitive picture is by no means simple. But the point is not overlooked in criticisms of restrictive practices.

To the extent that shippers who use the services of a particular conference to ship all their goods on the particular routes on which the conference operates receive a rebate in due course, it is that much more difficult, but by no means impossible, for a potential new entrant to break into the market. To the extent, though, that conferences do not use deferred rebate schemes (and there are many which do not), but do use their oligopoly power to raise the price of their services (so that it becomes greater than the long-run marginal cost of producing those services), it should not be difficult for a potential new entrant by charging a price for services lower than the conference tariff, to attract business to itself and ultimately to force the conference to adopt a new price system.

In this connection, one of the less rational policies of developed countries has been their explicit justification of, and support for, restrictive agreements in the field of shipping, even though such agreements are likely to lead to inefficiency and, in addition, encourage developing countries to resort increasingly to flag discrimination. With the massive extension of government intervention in industry and trade that has taken place since the Second World War there has become evident in recent years a conspicuous lack of coherence in the industrial and commercial policies of most major trading nations.[16] In policy discussion there has thus begun to develop a considerable literature on how to make policies for the provision of public assistance to private enterprise consistent with the principles of a market economy. And by "public assistance" is meant all forms of support ranging from direct subsidies to government procurement policies and acceptance of restrictive business practices.[17]

Several studies and reports have urged that in developing policies towards industries that are in competitive difficulty, a clear distinction should be drawn between "fair" or appropriate "adjustment assistance", on the one hand, and "unfair" or inappropriate government aid, on the other.

(a) Appropriate forms of assistance in a market economy aim at shifting resources out of industries that are no longer competitive.

(b) Inappropriate forms of assistance aim at keeping resources in an industry (through the provision of subsidized capital expenditures, subsidized research and development and subsidized skills) and are merely a substitute for traditional forms of protection.[18]

If such an approach to "problem" industries is to be adopted internationally, if only as part of a reformed "safeguard mechanism" (for providing emergency protection against sudden surges of imports of a particular product),[19] it could be difficult to justify the permanent exclusion of shipping (and air transport) from such a framework of policy discussion.

The major justification for the liner conference system in shipping – which was accepted uncritically by the Rochdale enquiry in Britain – is comparable with that which has been used with respect to other restrictive business practices. It is, as mentioned earlier, that it would be impossible for the industry, because of its very nature, to provide a regular service of such quality in the absence of a conference system which regulates freight rates. A detailed examination of the liner conference system would require a paper in itself. Suffice it to say at this point that no evidence has yet been produced to show that a service of a certain degree of quality for shippers could not be provided regularly, and at a lower price, in the absence of restrictive arrangements.

Without such evidence, it is inconsistent of governments of developed countries to criticize, on the one hand, the attempts of developing countries to break into the trade of certain routes by means of flag discrimination and subsidies and to support, on the other hand, restrictive arrangements among developed countries which are partly responsible for the actions of developing countries. A more constructive approach, in seeking to subject the former to some form of international regulation, would be to take steps towards making the liner conferences more open to the winds of international competition.

Need for Balanced Growth

One of the more fashionable theses regarding the path of economic development in developing countries in the post-war period has been that of "balanced" economic growth. Countries should not develop in a lopsided fashion with a disproportionate share of resources going to agriculture or exports, but should ensure that investment is taking place in a number of interrelated activities. The attempt therefore of countries with a low *per capita* income to achieve a faster rate of economic growth, as well as to diversify their output, has meant the development of national merchant marine fleets, national oil companies, national airways, national capital markets and nationalized banking and insurance. Unless specific resort is made to arguments regarding the external effects of particular industries, the notion of balanced growth makes very little economic sense. Following the desire to maximize their real income, countries should produce that combination of goods in which they have a comparative advantage, when the advantage is measured in social and not private terms. This almost certainly leads to the proposition that it would be extremely inefficient for all developing countries to develop such industries as merchant marine fleets and so on.

Short-term Capital Movements

One of the major developments in the international economy during the 1960s and subsequently has been the development of an international capital market in both short and long-term funds. The development of the markets, and especially the Euro-currency market, has resulted in an increased mobility of capital between countries and a greater sensitivity of capital movements to interest rate differentials. In commenting on the growth of these markets the IMF has observed that "perhaps the most important implications of the increased mobility of capital permitted and facilitated by the Euro-currency market and the international bond market are to be found in the challenges that they present to the effectiveness and independence of national monetary policies".[20]

In an international monetary system based on a gold-dollar standard, with exchange rates fixed to the dollar, the existence of an international capital market means that monetary policy actions taken by the United States are quickly transmitted to the rest of the world and will tend to render an individual country's monetary policy ineffective.[21] In general terms a country cannot pursue an independent monetary policy and maintain a fixed exchange rate.

During a period of restrictive monetary policy, companies and banks may borrow (lend) through the Euro-currency market, convert the funds into local foreign currency and therefore increase (decrease) the cash reserves of the banking system and of the domestic money supply. On the other hand, non-bank residents who are short of funds during a credit squeeze may either liquidate their position in the Euro-currency market or increase their borrowing in the market. "In all these instances, monetary policy actions may tend to prove self-defeating to the extent that they induce undesired capital inflows or outflows instead of the intended changes in total domestic borrowing and spending."[22]

The reaction by countries to this problem has been to impose controls or incentives or both to reduce the inflow and outflow of capital. If for example a country wished to pursue a tight money policy, then in the short run this would lead to an increase in interest rates and, *ceteris paribus,* an inflow of capital which would off-set the actions that it had undertaken by raising the stock of high-powered money and in turn the money supply. To avoid such repercussions, many countries find it convenient either to impose straightforward controls on the inflow of capital, or to tax those financial institutions or companies which attract such an inflow, so that it is no longer profitable for them to pay such high interest on a foreign held debt.

As a closing remark on this chapter, it might be mentioned that even if the discriminatory aspects of "invisible barriers to invisible trade" were to be eliminated, the domestic service would still have various intangibles in its favour, largely to do with consumer preferences for what is familiar, while foreign services take a while to familiarize themselves with local customs. After all, the greatest obstacle to those trying to penetrate the Japanese market, it is said, is the Japanese language. Obviously, such "constraints" vary from country to country and, too, from service to service.

NOTES

1. Harry G. Johnson, "Introduction" to Duncan Burn and Barbara Epstein, *Realities of Free Trade: Two Industry Studies* (London: Allen & Unwin, for the Trade Policy Research Centre, 1972), pp. xxii-xxiii.
2. See in particular Johnson, "Optimal Trade Interventions and Domestic Distortion", in Richard E. Caves, Johnson and Peter B. Kenan (eds), *Trade, Growth and the Balance of Payments* (Chicago: Rand McNally, 1964).
3. *Establishment or Expansion of Merchant Marines in Developing Countries*, Report of the UNCTAD Secretariat (New York: United Nations, 1968), paras 229 and 261.
4. *Ibid.*, para. 258.
5. Johnson, *op. cit.*
6. *The Jones Act* (Washington: Transportation Institute, 1966).
7. Quoted in *ibid.*
8. W. R. Malinowski, "European Insurance and the Third World", *Journal of World Trade Law,* London, August-September 1971.
9. See Report of the *Royal Commission on Banking and Finance* (Ottawa: Queen's Printer, 1965), ch.18, "An Approach to Banking Legislation", p.374.
10. *Ibid.*
11. *Ibid.*
12. *Ibid.*
13. *Establishment or Expansion of Merchant Marines in Developing Countries, op. cit.,* TD/26/Rev.1, para. 261, p.52.
14. S. G. Sturmey, *British Shipping and World Competition* (London: Athlone Press, 1962).
15. *Establishment or Expansion of Merchant Marines in Developing Countries, op. cit.,* para. 12, p.3.

16. The incoherence of government subsidies and other interventions has been underscored in Goran Ohlin, "Trade in a Non-Laissez-Faire World", in Paul A. Samuelson (ed.), *International Economic Relations* (London: Macmillan, for the International Economic Association, 1969).

17. For a general analysis of public subsidies, see Denton and O'Cleireacain, *op. cit.*, and a further study arising out of the same project, namely Denton, O'Cleireacain and Sally Ash, *Trade Effects of Public Subsidies to Private Enterprise* (London: Macmillan, for the Trade Policy Research Centre, 1975).

    An expression of public concern about the management of public subsidies can be found in *Public Money in the Private Sector*, Sixth Report of the Expenditure Committee of the House of Commons (London: HM Stationery Office, 1972), and the *Third Report of the Committee of Public Accounts: Session 1971-72*, House of Commons (London: HM Stationery Office, 1972).

18. In this connection, see Sir Alec Cairncross *et al.*, *Economic Policy for the European Community: The Way Forward* (London: Macmillan, for the Institut für Weltwirtschaft an der Universität Kiel, 1974), pp.122 *et seq.*

19. One of the most thorough analyses of the problems involved is Jan Tumlir, "Emergency Protection against Sharp Increases in Imports", in Hugh Corbet and Robert Jackson (eds), *In Search of a New World Economic Order* (London: Croom Helm, for the Trade Policy Research Centre, 1974).

20. IMF *Annual Report 1970, op. cit.*, p. 91.

21. There is now an extensive literature on this subject: Johnson, *Inflation and the Monetarist Controversy*, De Vries Lectures (Amsterdam: Elsevier, 1971), especially Lecture III on "The Monetarist Approach to Stabilization Policy in an Open Economy"; J. J. Polak, "Monetary Analysis of Income Formation and Payments Problems", *IMF Staff Papers*, vol. VI, 1957-58; Johnson, "The Monetary Approach to Balance-of-Payments Theory", in M. B. Connolly and A. K. Swoboda (eds), *International Economics: The Geneva Essays* (London: Allen & Unwin, 1972); Robert A. Mundell, "The International Distribution of Money in a Growing World Economy", *Monetary Theory: Inflation, Interest and Growth in the World Economy* (New York: Goodyear, 1971), ch. 15; A. Collery, "International Adjustment, Open Economies, and the Quality Theory of Money", *Princeton Studies in International Finance* (Princeton: Princeton University Press, 1971); and Karl Bruner, "Money Supply Process in an Open Economy", in Connolly and Swoboda (eds), *op. cit.*

22. IMF *Annual Report 1970, op. cit.*

CHAPTER 4

Global Approach to Constraints on Invisible Trade

The problems of constraints on international transactions in invisibles are of some concern to the General Agreement on Tariffs and Trade (GATT), the instrument by which the commerce of the free-enterprise world has been governed since the Second World War, helping to restore some semblance of order. They are of more concern, though, to UNCTAD. But by far the most important inter-governmental organization dealing with them is the OECD. To appraise the role which the OECD plays in this field it is necessary to understand the background and development of the Organization for European Economic Cooperation (OEEC) which preceded the OECD.[1]

From the viewpoint of free trade in goods and services, as well as the free flow of capital between countries, the inter-war years — and especially the Great Depression and its aftermath — were a most unsatisfactory period. As a result of rapidly falling export prices and of rising unemployment throughout the world, countries sought to improve their balance-of-payments positions and their reserve holdings (and in particular gold) in order to insulate themselves from the general depression in world trade. They imposed exchange controls on current and capital account transactions and introduced various non-tariff barriers to trade such as import quotas, customs valuation procedures and other administrative devices.[2]

During the Second World War, exchange control was extended by those countries which had introduced it, and adopted by almost all European countries. Restrictions over international transactions themselves were also made extremely severe. In the immediate post-war years the flow of goods, services and capital between countries in the international economy, and among West European countries in particular, was highly restricted. Payments between West European countries were subject to annually negotiated bilateral agreements, by which countries tried to balance their trade bilaterally by a restriction of payments to "hard" currency countries, especially the United States. The effects of these restrictions were not only to distort the pattern of trade and capital movements, but also to reduce the amount of trade taking place in the world as a whole.

In 1947 the OEEC was established to promote, with the help of Marshall aid, the reconstruction of Western Europe. Austria, Belgium, Denmark, France, Germany, Greece, Iceland, Ireland, Italy, Luxembourg, the Netherlands, Norway, Portugal, Spain, Sweden, Switzerland, Turkey and the United Kingdom were the members and Canada and the United States were associate members. Among other things, their objective was to "extend their commerce, reduce progressively barriers to trade among themselves . . . and restore or maintain the stability of their economies and general confidence in their national currencies".

One of the first achievements of the OEEC was the European Payments Union, which arranged credit facilities for member countries which found themselves with the problem of a balance-of-payments deficit, so that one of the major causes of discrimination between member countries was removed. One other important achievement was the acceptance by member countries of a Code of Liberalization of Invisible Transactions, which classified invisible trans-actions into four broad categories and included a list, within each category, of all of the transactions involved. It also subdivided transactions into those which countries were bound to liberalize and those which they were simply recommended to liberalize. The way in which the OEEC approached the liberalization of invisible trade was therefore to tackle simultaneously the problem of payments and the problem of transactions.

Since these initial measures, the OEEC further continued the process of liberalizing international transactions in invisibles when, in 1955, the member governments made the liveralization of all current invisibles obligatory, limiting in

time the right of countries to suspend liberalization when in
balance-of-payments difficulties. Two years later the OEEC
agreed that countries should undertake definite obligations to
liberalize restrictions on the movement of direct foreign
investment and other long-term capital movements. In 1959
the various obligations and recommendations that were
already in existence were set out in another "code of
liberalization" comparable with that for current invisible
operations.

In discussing its aims, the OECD has stated that it "has
taken over from the OEEC the two Codes for the Liberalization of Capital Movements and of Current Invisible
Operations,[3] the aim of which is to ensure the highest
attainable degree of freedom for transactions and transfers
between member countries in the fields of capital movements
and current operations. The Organization is also engaged in
cooperative activities designed to improve the capital markets
of member countries, with a view to increasing the avail-
ability of savings for investment and promoting balance-of-
payments equilibrium."[4]

At this point it should be noted that, whereas the OEEC
was principally a West European organization, the OECD
included as full members both the United States and Canada,
thus becoming more plainly an Atlantic endeavour. Later its
membership was extended to Japan, in 1960, and in the early
1970s to other Pacific countries, Australia and New Zealand.
Finland also joined in 1964.

Both the OECD Codes of Liberalization of Current
Invisible Operations and of Capital Movements (set out in
Appendices 1 and 2) have a great deal in common. The same
basic principle, that of complete liberalization of trade,
underlies both of them. Article 1 section (a) of both Codes
are as similar as they are basic: "Members shall eliminate
between one another . . . restrictions on current invisible
transactions and transfers" in one; and "Members shall
progressively abolish between one another . . . restrictions on
movements of capital to the extent necessary for effective
economic cooperation", in the other.[5] The Code of Liberalization of Capital Movement also has a specific section, stating
that "Members shall, in particular, endeavour:

(1) To treat all non-resident owned assets in the same way irrespective of the date of their formation, and

(2) To permit the liquidation of all non-resident owned assets or of their liquidation proceeds."[6]

Each also has an article making it explicit that liberalization should proceed on a non-discriminatory basis, and although the codes are drawn up on the basis of complete liberalization, provision nevertheless is made, first, for countries which cannot accept this principle without reserve to register their "reservations" and, secondly, for member countries who agree to accept the principle of complete liberalization, but who wish on a temporary basis to impose restrictions on transactions ("derogations") to do so, although in different circumstances these would be liberalized.

There are three main reasons for reservations. In the first place, some countries, while agreeing to the principle of complete liberalization, have found that in the case of particular transactions their internal legislation was in con-flict with the principle, since legislation exists which specifically provides for restrictions to be imposed under particular circumstances. Until such legislation was changed, they were obliged to lodge reservations. Many of the early reservations which were lodged with the OEEC were for this reason and hence were only temporary.

The second main reason for reservations relates to the desire of countries to protect particular industries. The main reservations operative under the OECD Code of Liberaliza-tion of Current Invisible Operations deal with transport, insurance and films, none of which appear to be temporary, but are plainly intended to protect these industries on a continuing basis.

Thirdly, there are some OECD countries which because of their general economic position, in particular their relatively low value of real GNP *per capita* by comparison with other West European countries, have argued that they are unable at their stage of development to accept the principle of complete liberalization. The liberalization obligations of the code on capital movements do not apply, for instance, to Greece, Iceland and Turkey. (And they did not apply to the overseas provinces of Portugal before their independence.)

The codes also make provision for countries which accept the principles of liberalization to derogate from their commitments if the country's "economic and financial situation justifies such a course". The two particular reasons which are mentioned are (i) if the measures of liberalization which had been taken resulted in "serious economic disturbance" and (ii) if the country's overall balance of payments deteriorates to such an extent that "drastic measures must be taken". If a country invokes a derogation clause, though, it has to be reviewed periodically by the OECD's Committee on Invisible Transactions and the restrictions must be imposed in such a way that they do not unnecessarily damage the economic interests of another member country.

Evaluation of OECD Measures

Judged by their objectives when they were first set up under the OEEC in the early 1950s, there can be little dispute that the OECD codes of liberalization have been a success in achieving a degree of liberalization of invisible transactions and long-term capital movements. The present degree of liberality in these types of international transactions, and the corresponding emphasis on multilateral rather than bilateral agreements, is far removed from the situation of the late 1940s. With the exception of a few particular industries in some West European countries, clearly being protected from foreign competition, there is almost complete freedom of trade in invisibles and a fair degree of freedom of long-term capital movements among the more developed countries in the OECD. All that said, there are grounds for arguing that, in meeting the problems of the present, the codes are only partially adequate.

In the first place, if one considers the problem of the distortion of invisible trade and capital movements as a *global* rather than either as a *regional* problem or as a problem concerning only highly developed countries (and from the evidence which exists this is inevitable), the fact that the OECD has a membership which is largely limited to the developed countries in the world is in this respect a serious disadvantage – even though this may be an important advantage as far as other matters are concerned. This disadvantage is inevitable in view of the fact that the OEEC was set up to solve the problems of trade distortion in Western Europe, and those between Western Europe and North America, not those of the world as it has subsequently developed. The restrictions which exist in this field are as much, if not more, a matter for concern between the developed and the developing countries as they are between the existing members of the OECD. Whether one takes the problems of flag discrimination, the restrictions on the activities of foreign banks, the prohibitions placed on citizens wishing to insure abroad, and the limitations on the extent to which the profits of various foreign concerns can be repatriated, the membership of the OECD is a very limited group of countries within which to seek a solution. This is in marked contrast to the membership of the GATT.

Secondly, even within the present system of liberalization, there are some limitations in certain particular areas on the extent to which the OECD can achieve this objective. Several examples can be given.

(i) Canada does not adhere to the Code of Liberalization of Capital Movements.

(ii) The United States does not accept the principle of liberalization as applicable to maritime freights. Note 1 to Annex A of the Code on Current Invisible Operations, which is a List of Current Invisible Operations, reads as follows:

> The provisions of C/1 "Maritime freights, including chartering, harbour expenses, disbursements for fishing vessels, et cetera", of C/5, first sub-paragraph, "For all means of maritime transport: harbour services (including bunkering and provisioning, maintenance, repairs, expenses for crews, etc.)", and of the other items that have a direct or indirect bearing on international maritime transport, are intended to give residents of one Member State the unrestricted opportunity to avail themselves of, and pay for, all services in con-

nection with international maritime transport which are offered by residents of any other Member State. As the shipping policy of the Governments of the Members is based on the principle of free circulation of shipping in international trade in free and fair competition, it follows that the freedom of transactions and transfers in connection with maritime transport should not be hampered by measures in the field of exchange control, by legislative provisions in favour of the national flag, by arrangements made by governmental or semi-governmental organisations giving preferential treatment to national flag ships, by preferential shipping clauses in trade agreements, by the operation of import and export licensing systems so as to influence the flag of the carrying ship, or by discriminatory port regulations or taxation measures — the aim always being that liberal and competitive commercial and shipping practices and procedures should be followed in international trade and normal commercial considerations should alone determine the method and flag of shipment.

The second sentence of this Note does not apply to the United States.

(iii) Primarily because of their stage of economic development, four of the least wealthy states — Greece, Iceland, Turkey and the overseas provinces of Portugal — are not obligated to the liberalizing requirements of the Code of Liberalization of Capital Movements.

(iv) In addition, various reservations invoked by nearly all countries dealing with road transport, films and insurance are still being maintained and show little sign of being withdrawn. It would appear that they are, in effect, permanent reservations.

(v) Greece, Turkey and the overseas provinces of Portugal are not obligated to the Code of Liberalization of Current Invisible Operations.

In the third place, certain member countries that have not imposed legal restraints on the movements of capital, which would technically require that reservations be lodged under the OECD code, have nevertheless introduced programmes of "voluntary" restraint and "guide-lines" on the movement of capital which are clearly contrary to the code. For example, the United States has only one reservation lodged in the OECD code on capital movements, either prohibiting direct investment in the United States by non-residents in such areas as fresh water shipping, domestic radio communications and domestic air transport or limiting to 25 per cent foreign participation in such corporations and in addition placing restrictions on foreign investment in coastal shipping, hydro-electric power production, other forms of communication and the utilization for production of atomic energy. But from 1963 to 1974 the United States applied various measures to reduce its balance-of-payments deficit which, although not lodged as reservations under the Code, were restrictive:

(a) Interest Equalization Tax (1964) to reduce the attractiveness of the American capital market to European borrowers by taxing them so that the interest cost in Western Europe and the United States would be equalized.

(b) The Foreign Direct Investment Programme, which placed limits on the outflow of capital by corporations for their own direct foreign investment abroad.

(c) The Voluntary Foreign Credit Restraint Programme, which aimed at limiting the capital outflow from banks and other financial institutions for lending and investment in foreign countries.

Fourthly, the OECD codes can to some extent be criticized for treating the symptoms, rather than the malaise, with respect to various barriers to invisible trade. The OECD approach to trade and capital liberalization is to tackle the problems of transactions. If a particular transaction cannot be made this in itself is treated as the restriction. But in many areas this approach fails to get at the real barriers to trade. For example, while Australia does not restrict her citizens from conducting business with foreign banks, and therefore as far as banking is concerned has complete liberalization under the OECD code, this does not reveal the fact that foreign banks are prohibited from setting up branches in Australia.

The conclusion which emerges in considering the present OECD codes of liberalization is that they are only partly suited to tackling constraints on invisible trade. In numerous ways, countries are able to get around the codes by policies of persuasion, rather than policies embodied in legislation. The codes are difficult to enforce and, in any case, the relatively small membership of the OECD means that it is not well placed to broach the global problems of restrictions on invisible trade.

Possible Forms of Action

It is important to consider the numerous types of policies which have from time to time been recommended. Although they are various they can be fairly easily categorized into five different types.

Retaliation

The crudest type of policy, which is more often than not advocated as a measure of last resort, and is frequently accompanied by a feeling of complete frustration, is that of straightforward retaliation. If a particular country forbids the entry to its country of British banks or British insurance companies or excludes the possibility of British ships carrying its trade, the United Kingdom should accord exactly the same treatment to that country's banks and insurance companies and ensure that the British Government requires British trade with other countries to be carried only in British ships and those of the other countries with which Britain is engaged in trade.

Three advantages are claimed for this type of action. First, it could be argued that, although a desperate measure, it is better than the inconclusiveness of diplomatic activity. Secondly, to the extent that it penalizes the country which has imposed restrictions, it might well produce a change in that country's policy. Thirdly, it might be a way, although not of increasing the United Kingdom's invisible exports, of inducing a switch by United Kingdom residents from purchasing invisible imports to buying British-produced invisibles, something which would show up in the balance-of-payments as an increase in the invisible surplus.

Retaliation, however, is an extremely short-sighted policy. While in the short term it may lead to an increase in British business, this could well be only the first round effect. Retaliation invites further retaliation, which from Britain's point of view could lead to even more restrictions being placed on her invisible exports. From a world point of view, if other countries pursued comparable retaliatory policies, it would lead to an escalation of individual countries' barriers to invisible trade, which would reduce the level and rate of growth of world trade in invisibles, which in the long run would be disadvantageous to all.

Bilateral Agreements

One approach to the problem might be for governments to make bilateral agreements with other governments so that barriers to trade between them could be reduced and possibly eliminated. If such an approach were adopted the number of agreements which would have to be negotiated in the world as a whole would be enormous. If there are 120 countries, then 7,140 ($120 \times 119 \div 2$) separate agreements would be needed! At first sight, given the constraints outlined, it seems particularly appealing that the United Kingdom should just go ahead and form agreements to reduce the barriers to trade with various countries over shipping, banking, insurance, direct foreign investment and so forth, reciprocity being made the basis of the agreements. In the field of banking, one could imagine a particular agreement between Australia or Canada and the United Kingdom whereby British banks would be allowed to establish in these countries. If the agreement proved difficult the United Kingdom could impose certain restrictions on Australian and Canadian banks in London.

The main objection to this type of solution, in which reciprocity was the basis of the bilateral agreement, is that it could easily be, in addition, an agreement that discriminated against third countries. From the point of view of the world as a whole, the result could be a multiplicity of agreements which, although based on the principle of reciprocity, nevertheless rejected the most-favoured-nation (MFN) principle which requires equal treatment and has been central to the GATT system of agreements in the field of international trade.[7]

GATT-Style Multilateral Negotiations

Another approach to the problem might be to have a multilateral system of agreements in the field of invisibles, comparable with that of the GATT in the field of traded goods. If such an approach as this were to be adopted, it would require that some inter-governmental organization, such as the GATT or the OECD or a new organization, should draw up an inventory of the types of constraints which exist in the field of invisibles. Secondly, some system of negotiation would have to be agreed on by the member countries. In the area of tariffs, the negotiation of tariff reductions is relatively easy because the effective rate of a tariff in one country can be easily compared with the effective rate in another, and because some attempt can be made to calculate the effects of tariff reductions on the country's trade. This enables negotiations to proceed on a reciprocal basis with "concessions" offered being balanced against "concessions" received. Measuring the effect of non-tariff barriers to visible trade, however, is difficult if not impossible. Negotiating on a reciprocal basis, interpreted in a narrow sense, is therefore out of the question. The same would be the case in respect of negotiations on "non-tariff barriers" to invisible trade. Just as with visible trade, the form of negotiations in the field of invisible trade might be a "barrier-by-barrier" approach, a group of "barriers" negotiated together or the negotiation, perhaps, of codes of conduct on the part of governments.

There are three main problems in trying to apply a GATT-style solution to the problem of the reduction of barriers in the field of invisibles: (i) that of reducing a heterogeneous set of barriers to trade to a manageable number, while at the same time ensuring that the major problems are being examined; (ii) devising a system for negotiation; and lastly (iii) ensuring that agreements are in fact enforced.

The problems with applying a GATT-style approach to the problems of invisibles can be seen in the problems the GATT already has in applying its own approach to tariff reductions in the field of non-tariff barriers. In attempting to draw up an inventory of government interventions, by asking countries to notify its Industrial Committee of other countries' constraints, the GATT found that the total number of complaints amounted to about eight hundred. These were later classified into thirty categories. In 1971 the GATT prepared to negotiate on three categories: (i) standards and their enforcement, (ii) quantitative restrictions and licensing and (iii) customs valuation.

In 1973 the Tokyo Round of multilateral GATT negotiations were formally launched covering *inter alia* non-tariff barriers to trade. The problems of agreeing on a negotiation procedure have been tentative and slow. Between the Kennedy and Tokyo rounds the method has essentially been barrier-by-barrier approach confined to areas in which countries are prepared to consider negotiation. Not surprisingly the pace of progress was painfully slow with only one or two of the list of thirty important non-tariff categories being dealt with each year. If anything, constraints on invisibles are even more heterogeneous than non-tariff barriers to visible trade; and if this type of approach were adopted, it would be extremely slow indeed.

The third problem is that of enforcement of agreements and of possible derogations. This is one of the weaknesses of the GATT, as it is indeed of the OECD in enforcing its codes of liberalization. The main way of dealing with countries which do not conform is simply to confront them with complaints about their violation of their obligations to GATT and then either to retaliate on an extremely limited basis, which is rare, or else for the parties concerned to negotiate a bilateral settlement which is acceptable to both while still being based on the MFN principle. To all intents and purposes, if barriers to invisible trade were to be part of a multilateral settlement, the enforcement of the results of the negotiations would have to rely on an appeal to national goodwill.

Codes of Conduct

Yet another possible approach would be for the countries concerned with invisible trade to draw up codes of conduct in each of the different areas covered by invisibles, embodying in as detailed a way as possible and on a multilateral basis, the principles of non-discrimination and reciprocity.[8] The principle of reciprocity would be satisfied through equal commitment to the codes, while the objectives of the principle of non-discrimination might be achieved, paradoxically, by basing the codes on agreements between the major trading countries and thereafter applying conditional MFN; which is to say, countries can only benefit from a code if they are a party to it (as is the case *de facto* with the GATT Anti-dumping Code) or if they are a party to a much wider agreement covering tariffs, non-tariff barriers and agricultural problems.[9]

Such codes would have to deal explicitly with the following types of problems:

(a) the role of government in the particular industry, covering such issues as the protection of deposits in banking and insurance, the role of governments in controlling liner conferences in shipping and the extent to which foreign ownership of manufacturing industry should be permitted;

(b) specific measures of liberalization and rules of procedure;

(c) the issue of subsidies, rather than discrimination, for infant industries;

(d) the "need" for particular industries, especially in relation to developing countries;

(e) the possibilities of derogation and the specific cases in which they may be used; and

(f) the method of enforcement of the measures of liberalization.

An example of a code which has something similar to those which might be envisaged in the field of invisibles is the GATT Anti-dumping Code which was agreed during the Kennedy Round negotiations (1964-7). This code defines dumping as a situation in which "the export price of the product exported from one country to another is less than the comparable price in the ordinary course of trade for the like product when destined for consumption in the exporting country".[10] Under the code a government may impose duties on the product being "dumped" in order to raise its price to the level of domestic producers. But, before a government can take action and impose anti-dumping duties and so protect its own producers against this kind of action, it has to show that they are suffering "material injury"[11] and not simply from the forces of normal competition.

The difference between agreement on a code of behaviour and multilateral negotiations is important, involving as it does a difference of principle, not simply a difference in detail. The principle underlying multilateral negotiations is that of bargaining. In the field of tariffs in the past, concessions on one set of tariffs are traded off against concessions on another. The aim of a code, however, is not bargaining but a general acceptance by member countries of the principle embodied in the code. In the GATT Anti-dumping Code, the accepted principle is that dumping is harmful and should, on sufficient evidence of its existence, be countered by the actions of governments.

Unilateral Action

One approach to the problems of barriers to trade which, although not global in design, might nevertheless be significant in its effect would be for the United Kingdom unilaterally to remove various direct as well as indirect barriers to invisible trade which it is in its power to do. The obvious issues for consideration would be the abolition of exchange-control restrictions, the application of existing law on monopolies and restrictive practices to the case of shipping and the liberalization of restrictions connected with films. Governments, though, are not given to unilateral actions, even if they would be in their citizens' welfare.

General Code on Invisibles and Capital Movements

So far this book has argued that greater freedom of trade in the field of invisibles, and a greater liberalization of capital movements between countries, is desirable from the viewpoint of the world economy and that the plethora of existing constraints can only be adequately tackled on a global basis. Given the possible approaches just outlined, the most preferable development would be the drawing up of a general code on invisible and capital movements by the governments of countries with an interest in invisible trade and capital movements. If such a general code were to be successful in reducing various non-tariff barriers to invisible trade, certain features would be essential.

First, any government could become a signatory; indeed it would be essential that adherence to the code should include not only the developed but also the less developed countries. In this respect it would be superior to either the OECD or UNCTAD and more comparable with the GATT. Secondly, the code must be comprehensive, covering *inter alia* banking, insurance, commodity trading, royalties, brokerage, tourism, civil aviation, shipping, direct and portfolio investment. Thirdly, the code should not only deal with conventional non-tariff barriers to trade: it should also deal with restrictive practices on an international basis (which is critical to civil aviation and shipping at present). And, in the section dealing with capital movements, it should deal with balance-of-payments adjustment policy in the context of the reform of the international monetary system. A fourth feature would be the setting up of an institution to conduct the initial drafting of the code and any subsequent revisions; and, too, to arbitrate on conflicting interpretations of the Code and to adjudicate on infringements. Arbitration should be conducted by outside parties and could be organized on a national and international basis, depending on the issues.[12] Finally, the Code should be enforced either through a system of fines or through the withdrawal of privileges from a recalcitrant member.[13]

In order to make the concept of a general code more explicit and realistic, it is worth outlining the way in which it might cover three key areas. One activity from each of these areas has been selected to show the kinds of subjects it should cover: (i) financial services — banking; (ii) transport — shipping; and (iii) portfolio investment — short-term capital movements.

Financial Services: Banking

Although the term financial services covers a heterogeneous set of activities, from a policy standpoint they have many features and problems in common. The field of banking might serve to illustrate the coverage of a code. It would cover the following types of problems:

(a) The removal of discrimination between national and foreign banks with respect to the conditions for entry into banking (retail and wholesale): in particular, minimum capital requirements; cash and, if necessary, liquid ratios (to protect depositors); various controls on asset structure (for example, public/private sector lending, extent of lending to various sectors); restrictions on the maximum rate of interest payable on deposits and charged on loans.

(b) The precise relationship between foreign banks and the domestic law relating to banking; and, in particular, the relationship between different techniques of monetary control, especially "moral suasion" and foreign banks.

(c) The extent to which foreign banks in all countries should be exempt from certain requirements, such as cash and liquid asset reserve requirements and the maintenance of capital/deposit ratios, because they are branches of large banks, which maintain adequate reserves and capital through their head office.

(d) The extent to which monetary authorities should be permitted in the imposition of reserve requirements to discriminate between foreign and domestic owned deposits.

Transport: Shipping

Any discussion of codes of conduct applicable to international transportation is of necessity complicated, not only because governments are already involved in the fields of shipping and air transport in subsidizing these activities and providing them with various forms of protection, but also because of the existence of international agreements (the system of liner conferences and IATA) which have specifically set out to limit the extent of price competition.

A major discussion took place at the third UNCTAD, in Santiago, on various codes of conduct that might be applicable to the liner conference system in shipping. It appears that both the major participants, the developed countries (whose interests are mainly represented by the Committee of European National Shipowners Association [CENSA]) and the less developed countries, accepted the principle of the conference system and the need for a code of conduct to influence its operation. Such a code would deal *inter alia* with the following points:

(1) *Relations between the member lines of the conference:*

    (a) membership — criteria for admission, withdrawal and expulsion of members;

    (b) share of trade;

    (c) cargo and revenue pooling agreements;

    (d) sanctions against breaches of agreement by members;

    (e) machinery for self-policing; and

    (f) publication of conference practices.

(2) *Relations with shippers:*

    (a) Loyalty arrangements, such as the dual rate system, the contract system and the deferred rebates system;

    (b) dispensation to "loyal" shippers to use non-conference system;

    (c) publication of charges and regulations; and

    (d) consultation machinery, including representation of shippers on conference committees.

(3) *Freight rates:*

    (a) consultation regarding the determination of freight rate increases;

    (b) procedure for determining freight rates on new cargo;

(c) consultation regarding the imposition of surcharges; and

(d) procedures regarding freight rates as a result of devaluations, revaluations and floating currencies.

(4) *Other matters:*

(a) methods of restricting outside competition, such as the "fighting ship";

(b) the cross-subsidization through the present practice of averaging;

(c) the quality of service, in terms of cargo handling facilities, age and speed of ship and so on; and

(d) adequacy of service, in terms of providing the regularity desired by the particular trade.

(5) *Provision and machinery for implementation:*

(a) procedure for settling disputes which would be economical, impartial and easily accessible for all; and

(b) cover such issues as refusal of entry to conferences, increases in freight rates and loyalty agreements.

Four different codes were put forward at the Santiago meeting: (i) the OECD proposals, (ii) a report from the UNCTAD Secretariat, (iii) the Latin American draft and (iv) the Afro-Asian draft. The principal differences between the various proposals related to (a) the extent of government regulation in the international shipping industry, (b) the method of settling disputes, (c) the criteria of cargo sharing and (d) the basis on which new members may be admitted to a conference.

Broadly speaking, the developed countries, the major shipowners in the world, want as little government intervention as possible, the sharing of trade on a commercial basis, the admission of new members to be decided by existing shipowners (and then only if they can produce evidence of their commercial viability in shipping) and the settlement of disputes between members and also between shippers and shipowners with as little formal machinery and outside influence as possible.

On the other hand, the less developed countries are concerned to develop a new structure of world shipping in which the fleets of developing countries play "an increasing and substantial role";[15] to involve their governments both in implementing the code and in regulating shipping, to ensure that trade is shared on an equal basis if there are no third-country carrier participants, and to claim 80 per cent of the total trade even if there are third country carriers; to open conferences to shipping lines whose trade, including way port trade, is covered by that conference; to settle local and international disputes by arbitration and appeal to an impartial third party; to set up specific procedures for negotiation over rate increases and promotional freight rates; and to disallow deferred rebates and dual rate agreements subject to a fixed percentage between the contract and non-contract rates.

The fact that the less developed countries presented two draft codes was the result of disagreement on the role governments should play and on the form which arbitration should take. Since the beginning of the 1960s certain Latin American countries, and especially Brazil, have expanded their shipping industry as a consequence of cargo reservation and considerable government involvement in the liner conference system. As a consequence, the Latin American draft argued that "developing countries have the right to *protect* and promote their national merchant marines and that the measures adopted to this end will neither be considered discriminatory or given place to retaliation", whereas the Afro-Asian draft was much closer to that of the UNCTAD Secretariat. Highlighting this difference was the approach to arbitration as a way of dealing with parties which broke the code. While the Latin American proposals provided for local arbitration, any result of arbitration would require a final decision from the government of the country from which the cargo originated. By comparison the Afro-Asian draft proposed an arbitration system at a local level for local rates and other questions and, at an international level, for general rate changes which were binding on the parties concerned.

From an economic point of view, all of the proposals which have been put forward for a code of conduct for shipping, suffer a serious defect: namely, the acceptance of restrictive agreements and the exclusion of free competition as a basis for world liner shipping. As a result, the codes are not only concerned with the role that governments would play in relation to shipping, but also with the establishment of a set of rules to regulate an agreement, albeit one in which the two major groups have substantially different interests. There can be little doubt that developments in the direction of extending the restrictive practice can only lead to greater inefficiency. It cannot be emphasized enough that what is needed in this field is the transformation of restrictive agreements into arrangements based on liberal trade principles. This could be done by countries bringing shipping practices under their anti-trust or restrictive practices legislation with appropriate provisions for adjustment assistance.[16]

There seems little likelihood, though, of this solution being achieved, given the present pronouncements of the UNCTAD Secretariat, founded as they are on the twin principles of discrimination and an almost total disregard for global economic efficiency. In view of this, the code put forward by the OECD is far superior to the others in that it attempts to reduce the administrative costs of organizing shipping conferences, to admit new members only if they can prove their commercial viability and to share trade more on the basis of the shipowners' efficiency in providing the services rather than some arbitrary rule of thumb.

Portfolio Capital

A code of conduct in respect of portfolio investment is very much bound up with discussion on the future of the international monetary system. In particular, the subjects that should be dealt with by a code are dependent on the extent of exchange-rate flexibility between countries. In an ideal situation with flexible exchange rates, the subject of such a code would be restricted to matters like differential tax rates on foreign banks, the harmonization of conditions of entry for foreigners in domestic capital markets *et cetera*. In a world of less than fully flexible rates, however, such a code would deal *inter alia* with the following:

(a) the conditions under which restrictions on capital movements were justified (for example, to maintain interest rate differentials, to maintain an independent monetary policy, to avoid a speculative crisis);

(b) the type of restrictions which countries might impose in particular circumstances (for example special reserve requirements on foreign held or denominated deposits);

(c) the conditions for the issue of foreign bonds in the domestic capital market;

(d) harmonization of taxation systems which affect capital movements; and

(e) the conditions under which foreign exchange-rate changes are permissible.

Policy for Broaching Constraints on Invisibles

Free competition in the rendering of services in international business is one of the objectives of the OECD. Member countries have accepted among themselves quite definite commitments in respect of invisible transactions and transfers. Rules are laid down in two OECD codes. Provisions are made for temporary derogations from obligations – either through reservations, in specific types of invisible transaction, or more generally through escape clauses in emergency situations.

Even so, the liberalization of constraints on invisible trade has not come to occupy an important place in inter-governmental relations, in the sense that the liberalization of visible trade has done in the post-war period. Nor is there much likelihood of the situation changing in the course of the Tokyo Round of multilateral GATT negotiations. If those negotiations can be brought to a successful conclusion, there is some prospect though of constraints on invisible earnings becoming a matter of priority in subsequent GATT discussions, given the rapid integration of the world economy.

In the United States, the Trade Act of 1974, which defines the Administration's negotiating authority for the Tokyo Round negotiations, services are explicitly linked with merchandise trade in referring to distortions of inter-national competition. Quite plainly, the Administration has begun preparing Congress for negotiations with other countries in the field of services, if only in the wake of the Tokyo Round discussions. In this respect, it might be noted that, in a sense, if the Tokyo Round discussions succeed they will never end. For what many envisage is a more or less continuous process of consultation and negotiation on non-tariff interferences in international visible trade, particu-larly if agreement is reached on the substantial elimination of industrial stages (perhaps in two stages and over a decade or so), and on cases where emergency protection is being sought where sudden surges of imports of specific products are disrupting markets.

Rey Report and Services

In 1972 the High-level Group on Trade and Related Problems, established the year before by the OECD to advise governments on the development of international economic relations, only devoted a few pages in its report to the subject of "services". What the group, under the chairmanship of Jean Rey, formerly President of the Commission of the European Community, had to say is nevertheless worth recalling.[17]

The Report urged that action should be taken by the developed countries to ensure liberalization and non-discrimination in the services sector. It stressed the need for action in the fields of insurance, tourism and transport, particularly in shipping and air transport. The Rey Report added that, as in the case of goods, the developing countries should be allowed a limited time to adapt before undertaking full commitments. In specific fields it recommended in the following vein:

Insurance probably deserves first attention, the Rey Report suggested, not only because of its economic significance, but also because more than elsewhere progress towards real liberalization is held up by involved technical arguments. The rules of the Code of Liberalization of Current Invisible Operations concerning direct insurance transactions are incomplete and there are, moreover, numerous reservations on liberalized operations (including insurance relating to goods in international trade), because the authorities of a number of member countries are opposed to liberaliza- tion as long as there is no international harmonization of national insurance control regulations. These countries maintain, the report continued, that without such harmonization, conditions of international com- petition would be distorted. This is disputed by other member countries which have in fact liberalized without ill effects. The advantages for trade and industry of a progressive liberalization of the international insurance market are such, not least in the context of inflation, that the question should be re-examined with some urgency, the Rey Group concluded.

In the field of air transport, the report said, there is little prospect of multilateral and genuine international competition as long as governments wish to protect their national airlines, partly to safeguard their purely domestic requirements and partly for reasons of prestige, and to this end bargain bilaterally with other countries on landing rights, transit rights and the rights to pick up and set down passengers and freight. This unsatisfactory situation stems from technical and political issues which have defied solution for many years. In the interest of early liberalization a new impetus should be given to multilateral discussions. This might best done in a world-wide forum like the International Civil Aviation Organization, a specialized agency of the United Nations which was established in 1946. If necessary, the OECD would constitute an alternative institution for policy considerations in this field, the report suggested.

Transactions and transfers relating to maritime trans- port are free in principle, and liberalization is reinforced by a special Note in the Code which lists a variety of measures that are incompatible with "free and fair competition" and emphasizes that "normal commercial considerations should alone determine the method and

flag of shipment". When the United States joined the
Organization in 1960, the report recalled, it was unable
to subscribe to these principles and to assume an
obligation to free completely the choice of flag in their
foreign commerce. Other restrictive practices are maintained by governments or international shipping
companies. The status of the liberalization rule which
other OECD member countries consider to be of
paramount importance is thus weakened. This unsatisfactory situation has a bearing on the growing
difficulties which liberalization, desirable on a world-
wide basis, also meets as a result of flag discrimination
by the developing countries.

Tourism is liberalized under the OECD Code and
under normal circumstances the situation is satisfactory.
Here the Rey Report observed, however, that when
member countries are in balance-of-payments
difficulties and feel obliged to introduce restrictions, the
tourist allocation is often the first to be cut, and that
this has unfortunate consequences in that the burden is
to some extent shifted to countries which are also not in
a strong balance-of-payments position and for which
tourist revenue plays a significant role. The existing
procedure for the examination by the OECD of any
invocations of the balance-of-payments derogation
clause of the Code in respect of tourism ought to be
more rigorously applied in future. It should be brought
in line with the general approach to balance-of-
payments adjustment, the report insisted, the objective
being that member countries commit themselves not to
place limitations on the amount of foreign currency
available to tourists, other than in exceptional cases and
under clearly determined conditions.

McFadzean Report and Earnings from Investments

Turning to that component of invisibles which covers
"interest, dividends, profits and royalties", the basic question
concerns the freedom of international transactions in the
capital assets on which these represent the returns to the
investor. Published almost concurrently with the Rey Report

was a report (the McFadzean Report) of an advisory group of the Trade Policy Research Centre in London, which recalled the conventional view, developed from the experience of the 1930s and in the period since the Second World War, that freedom of trade in goods is beneficial, but freedom of trade in securities is a source of trouble that needs to be interfered with by official controls on international capital movements and investment. This view reflects the fact that it is primarily private individuals who bear the brunt of sudden changes in the flow of goods, and primarily central banks and treasuries that have to cope with the effects of international capital movements on their balances of payments at fixed exchange rates. In recent years, also, with the growth of the operations of multinational enterprises, there has come to be widespread popular suspicion and distrust of direct foreign investment and a belief that something should be done to control it.[18]

In both cases — portfolio capital movements and direct foreign investment — belief in the need for control has been clearly associated with the defects of the international monetary system. The lack of exchange-rate flexibility has provided an environment conducive to "speculative" capital movements which have been embarrassing to national monetary authorities. It has led to capital flows of direct investment in response to relative currency over-valuations and under-valuations which have possibly been unjustifiable in the light of long-run considerations of profitability and have certainly been awkward for monetary managers. Again, progress is dependent on improvement in the world's monetary system, so that intervention in international capital movements on balance-of-payments grounds are rendered unnecessary.

The improvement in question would permit an international agreement to prohibit interventions on the invisible side of the current account (for instance, regulations requiring repatriation of earnings, on the one hand, and blockage of repatriation of earnings by exchange controls, on the other). Such an agreement should be part of the negotiations for freer trade, the McFadzean Report argued, although it would require a different group of experts that have hitherto taken little or no part in trade negotiations.

The larger question, however, concerns the freedom of capital movements themselves. The multinational enterprise is a special agency of such movements. On the broader question of capital movements in general, there is a general case for freedom of capital movement as a more efficient method of achieving the methods of freedom of trade, since capital has to move to labour only once while traded goods have to keep moving. There is an exception that arises if rates of taxation on capital differ greatly between countries. In that case capital may move to countries where its social, as distinct from its private, returns (the social including the taxes) is lower where it goes than it was where it came from. In practice this does not seem to be an important problem, but if governments find it is, it would be more efficient for them to remove the distorting fiscal influences unilaterally or by negotiation than to retain the distortions and seek to counter their influence by imposing controls on capital movements.

The McFadzean Report therefore suggested that multilateral GATT negotiations should at least have on the agenda consideration and discussion of the interactions among trade, foreign investment and invisible earnings with a view to reaching agreement on possible principles and procedures for liberalizing trade in capital assets and the international flow of earnings on them. In a sense, rules on invisible transactions would provide a link, institutionally, between the regulation of commercial and monetary policies that on much broader grounds seems necessary for the greater efficiency of the world economy.

Thus, to conclude, the problem of the removal of constraints to trade in the field of invisibles must be seen as the focal point of two conceptually separate, but none the less interrelated, problems, namely those of

(a) the liberalization of trade between companies in services, such as banking, insurance, brokerage, transport *et cetera,* and

(b) the removal of restrictions to the free flow of direct and portfolio investment.

Governments should continue to aim for the liberalization of trade in invisibles and should therefore not attempt retaliatory action against particular countries or attempt bilateral agreements which discriminate against third countries. The problem of trade liberalization is global; it cannot be emphasized enough that it is neither bilateral nor regional. For any such liberalization to have a chance of success, the governments must be prepared to change their policies toward international restrictive agreements.

At a global level, it would be virtually impossible for the government to attack the problem in terms of the GATT's current barrier-by-barrier approach, because the constraints to invisible trade are so heterogeneous. In this respect the problem of trade liberalization in the field of invisibles is quite different from that of visibles. A better approach would be to negotiate a General Code on Invisibles and Capital Movements that would need to be established in an institutional framework (which might in fact be an extension of an existing one). This General Code would parallel in the field of invisible trade the work of the GATT in the field of visible trade.

For this approach, or any other, to succeed it would be necessary for a considerable degree of political will to be generated, perhaps initially through the OECD and thence through the GATT. That political will might be induced if the OECD was to initiate and maintain an inventory of constraints on invisible transactions. This would in any case be necessary in order to demonstrate the size of the problem and to provide a basis for inter-governmental discussions.

In negotiating the General Code, the first objective should be to secure the commitment of governments. On tariffs it is possible for governments to make once-for-all decisions. But on measures that are part and parcel of more intricate policies, having social and various other objectives, governments can only be expected to conform to international obligations over an extended period. An incrementalist approach is therefore necessary in pursuing the second objective which would need to be the elaboration of articles of the General Code on specific types of constraint. In the course of those discussions, and by a continuing process of consultation and negotiation, it should be possible gradually to secure adherence to the General Code — making use, where necessary, of its provisions for complaints and arbitration.

The momentum to carry forward a General Code on Invisibles and Capital Movements might be derived from the effort to reform the international trade and monetary system in response to chronic inflation, commodity shortages and the "energy crisis". If the approach outlined in these pages seems too prosaic, or not dramatic enough, there are some words of Harry Johnson that might be quoted:[19]

"Newspapers sell on headlines and popular biographies sell on prurient details of lurid lives. But societies function and prosper on the foundation of millions of citizens who commit neither burglaries nor rape nor slaughter on the highways, who commit neither assault with intent nor outright murder, and who attempt to live continuously as best they can at peace with their neighbours. More appropriately, it was not the famous outlaws still heralded in American 'westerns', but the countless and nameless unremembered settlers who civilized the Wild West (and for that matter tamed the outlaws themselves). The establishment of economic integration among a group of nation-states is a matter of establishing a civilized economic community. which involves taming the outlaw forces of protectionism and, what becomes more of a problem as integration proceeds, controlling the confidence men who attempt to sell covert protectionism as overt conformity with the principles of economic integration."

NOTES

1. For an account of the OECD and its predecessor, see Henry G. Aubrey, *Atlantic Economic Cooperation: The Case of the OECD* (New York: Praeger, for the Council on Foreign Relations, 1967).
2. See Bidwell, *op. cit.*
3. The main sections of these codes are reproduced in Appendices 2 and 3.
4. *OECD History, Aims and Structure* (Paris: OECD Secretariat, 1971).
5. *Ibid.*

6. *Ibid.*
7. Under Article 1 of the General Agreement, any concession negotiated between two or more countries must be extended *unconditionally* to all other signatory countries, except under certain conditions laid down in Article 24, which provides for the formation of free trade associations and customs unions, and in certain other circumstances.
8. On the subject of codes of conduct in the field of non-tariff barriers to visible trade, see Gerard and Victoria Curzon, *Hidden Barriers to International Trade*, Thames Essay No. 1 (1970), and *Global Assault to Non-tariff Trade Barriers*, Thames Essay No. 3 (London: Trade Policy Research Centre, 1972).
9. A conditional MFN approach to multilateral trade negotiations has been urged in Frank McFadzean *et al., Towards an Open World Economy,* Report of an Advisory Group (London: Macmillan, for the Trade Policy Research Centre, 1972), pp. 31-4. See the background paper to the McFadzean Report, published in the same volume, by Hugh Corbet, "Position of the MFN Principle in Future Trade Negotiations", pp. 157-67.
10. Curzon and Curzon, *Hidden Barriers to International Trade, op. cit.,* pp. 34-6.
11. *Ibid.*
12. For a discussion, in another context, of how a complaints and arbitration procedure might be operated, see Jan Tumlir, "Emergency Protection against Sharp Increases in Imports", in Corbet and Robert Jackson (eds), *In Search of a New World Economic Order* (London: Croom Helm, for the Trade Policy Research Centre, 1974), pp. 274 *et seq.* The paper deals with the reform of the "escape clause" provisions of the GATT.
13. Curzon and Curzon, *Global Assault on Non-tariff Trade Barriers, op. cit.,* pp. 5-10.
14. The various proposals are given in the following UNCTAD papers: *Code of Conduct for Liner Conference System,* TD/128 (New York: United Nations, 1971); *The Regulation of Liner Conferences,* TD/104 (New York: United Nations, 1971); and *International Shipping Legislation,* Report of the Working Group on International Shipping Legislation on its Third Session, TD/B/C.4/93, TD/B/C.4/154/12 (New York: United Nations, 1972).
15. *Preliminary Draft Code of Conduct for Liner Conferences Submitted by Argentina, Brazil, Colombia, Chile and Mexico,* Annex 1, TD/B/C.4/93. TD/B/C.4/15L/12. (New York: United Nations, 1972), Appendix 1, p. 1.
16. In the United Kingdom, the Office of Fair Trading has issued, at the time of writing, a notice of intention to place a draft Order before Parliament bringing service industries within the restrictive trade practice provisions of the Fair Trading Act, but excluding international shipping. In the European Community, the Commission appears to be taking the view, following a judgment of the

European Court in April 1973, that Articles 85 and 86 of the Treaty of Rome, dealing with restrictive business practices and monopolies, have a general application to shipping, although there is also in the Commission a contrary view.

17. High-level Group on Trade and Related Problems, *Policy Perspectives for International Trade and Economic Relations*, Rey Report (Paris: OECD Secretariat, 1972), pp. 77-80.

18. McFadzean *et al., op. cit.*, pp. 21-4.

19. Johnson, "Lessons of EFTA Experience in a Global Context", introduction to V. Curzon, *The Essentials of Economic Integration* (London: Macmillan, for the Trade Policy Research Centre, 1974).

Illustrative List of Discriminatory Constraints on Invisible Earnings

Before the problem of barriers to invisible trade can be discussed within a framework of economic policy, it is important to know, in as much detail as possible, the nature of the discriminatory constraints on the invisible earnings of non-nationals that are evident in the policies and practices of governments. The compilation of a comprehensive and exhaustive inventory of constraints would be such an enormous task that it could only be undertaken as a separate enquiry and with considerable resources and official backing.

The list below is not therefore meant to provide a systematic coverage of all barriers to invisible trade. There is another caveat that should be entered on the examples cited in this study. Government measures are always subject to change. In a period of international monetary turmoil, however, they are subject to a greater degree of change than usual. Although the specific instances cited above and below are correct at the time of writing, they may well be withdrawn or intensified or otherwise varied, which is to say they should be regarded as illustrative of a general state of affairs.

While the illustrative list covers many of the most important barriers, neither the list of countries, nor the types of constraints, is complete. The five major areas covered are banking, direct investment, insurance, shipping and travel. The list is divided between OECD countries and developing ones.

One notable omission from the illustrations is portfolio investment, but if this was covered properly it would have required a major study in itself, for the restrictions on foreign borrowing and lending (in many cases different for residents, non-residents, consumers, banks and corporations) are not

only very detailed; they are also changed very frequently to
meet the needs of monetary policy. Details of restrictions in
this field can, however, be found in the IMF annual
publication on exchange restrictions.

The list has been compiled from numerous sources. The
initial source was a questionnaire which was sent to the
economic sections of the London embassies of 80 countries.
The response was poor both in numbers and quality.
Information was therefore gleaned from: Appendix 4 of the
Report of the Committee of Inquiry in Shipping, (the
Rochdale Report, Cmnd, 4337), in the United Kingdom in
which is listed the "Details of Main Provisions Involving Flag
Discrimination in Force or Contemplated by Certain
Countries at 31 October 1969"; the report of the Inter-
national Chamber of Commerce on flag discrimination
published in 1969; the UNCTAD *Study on Insurance
Legislation and Supervision in Developing Countries*
(document TD/B/C.3/84, TD/B/C.3/AC.5/1); *Supervision of
Private Insurance in Europe* published by the OECD
Secretariat; and the OECD codes of liberalization of current
invisible operations and capital movements. Then there was
generous help from the British Insurance Association, the
United Kingdom Chamber of Shipping, Barclays Bank and
the First National City Bank of New York, but they bear no
responsibility for any judgments that are either implicit or
explicit in the illustrations.

BANKING: OECD Countries

Country	Area	Restrictions
Australia	New branches	New commercial banks (trading banks) and branches of overseas banks can be established only with the permission of the government. However, there has been an absolute ban on new banks since 1942. Representative offices and merchant banks are permitted.
	Repatriation of profits	No restrictions on current earnings but all transfers of capital require approval. However, no advance commitment to approve the request is given.

Country	Area	Restrictions
Austria	New branches	New branches or subsidiaries are not likely to receive approval, although new representative offices are permitted.
	Employment Regulations	Work permits are infrequently issued to non-residents.
Canada	New branches	Foreign equity participation in banking is limited to 25%.
	Employment regulations	Foreign employees must hold a work permit, the emphasis being on the employment of Canadian nationals.
Denmark	New branches	The establishment of a foreign-owned bank, subsidiary or branch except from another EEC country, is not permitted.
France	Asset portfolio controls	10% of domestic currency liabilities such as sight deposits, time deposits up to 3 years, and sundry accounts, must be kept daily in rediscountable medium-term bills. This restriction does not apply to branch banks.
Ireland	Repatriation of profits	Bank profits (as a percentage of the capital employed) are advised to fall between 19-22% gross (9-11% net). Profits can be repatriated without limitation, provided general exchange controls are observed.
	Employment regulations	Work permits are necessary for all non-EEC-member nationals. Unofficially, all banks incorporated in Ireland are encouraged to have a majority of Irish directors.
Italy	New branches	The establishment of new branches is permitted subject to authorization, which is generally given. However, the necessary foreign exchange licence is infrequently granted.

Country	Area	Restrictions
Japan	New branches	A licence is necessary to establish new branches, which is infrequently granted. New foreign banks are prohibited from entering retail banking.
	Interest payments and deposits	The central bank's rediscount facilities for export transactions are not extended to foreign banks. The central bank imposes quotas to restrict foreign branch banks from obtaining yen funds with foreign currencies converted through swap transactions or with increased free yen deposits. The overall foreign currency of any exchange bank operating in Japan is restricted to the quota prescribed by the central bank.
Netherlands	New branches	The expansion of existing banks is contingent on the level of domestic currency deposits, subject to the Netherlands Bank Act.
New Zealand	New branches	The establishment of new branches is permitted only in non-banking operations.
Switzerland	New branches	Foreign banks require the approval of the Federal Banking Commission. Approval is granted if the applicant's country grants reciprocal rights and has comparable restrictions within their banking system. The bank must not have underlying Swiss ownership and the authorities may request information about the identity of the bank's shareholders. The bank must abide by Swiss credit and monetary policy.
	Capital requirements	Full bank status requires a minimum ratio of permanent capital of 2m francs.
	Employment regulations	Work permits are required for foreigners, which are infrequently issued.

Country	Area	Restrictions
United States	New branches	The establishment of a new bank is permitted subject to the authorization of the individual state's banking authority and the Federal Reserve. Subsequent branching *within* the individual state is restricted except in the states of New York, California, Florida, Illinois and Massachusetts. The Bank Holding Act restricts acquisition of offices *outside* the individual state in which the bank is incorporated, as well as prohibiting subsidiaries. Branches of foreign banks conducting inter-state trade (Edge Act branches) are prohibited.

BANKING: Developing Countries

Country	Area	Restrictions
Argentina	New branches	The establishment of new branches or subsidiaries is prohibited.
Brazil	New branches	Authorization for the establishment of new branches of both foreign and domestic banks is suspended until the end of 1976. Foreign banks may purchase a minority holding in existing domestic banks or open representative offices, subject to authorization.
	Repatriation of profits	Up to 12% of the existing capital and reinvestment funds may be remitted abroad. Amounts exceeding this limit are subject to a progressive corporation tax ranging from 65–85% of the excess funds.
	Employment regulations	A minimum of two-thirds of those employed must be nationals.
Cyprus	Repatriation of profits	Profits, dividends and interest from approved investments may be transferred abroad after payment of any

Country	Area	Restrictions
Cyprus— continued		charges or taxes due, subject to approval.
	Employment regulations	Foreigners must hold labour permits.
Ghana	New branches	The central bank must approve the establishment of any new branch. Many financial activities are not open to foreign banks.
	Capital requirements	The minimum capital necessary for a foreign bank is 2m cedi or 5% of deposit liabilities, whichever is greater.
	Asset portfolio controls	The financing of export business is restricted.
	Repatriation of profits	Varying percentages of profits must be retained in a reserve fund. Remittance of profits is subject to approval, which is infrequently given.
	Employment regulations	Foreigners must hold work permits, the granting of which is subject to a quota.
Indonesia	New branches	New branches are not permitted, although representative offices can be established. The representative offices may not be engaged in any form of commercial banking.
India	New branches	The establishment of new branches of existing banks or new foreign banks is prohibited.
Iran	New branches	Representative offices may be established, although foreign participation exceeding 35% is not permitted.
	Repatriation of profits	A permit is required for the transfer of profits.
Jordan	Repatriation of profits	Profits from approved foreign investments may be remitted without limitation in the currency of the original investment after twelve months, subject to the approval of the Central Bank.

Country	Area	Restrictions
Kenya	Capital requirements	An additional K£400,000 of capital plus 5% assigned capital is required to be held by foreign banks.
	Employment regulations	Foreign personnel must hold work permits.
Lebanon	New branches	Representative offices are prohibited from operating in commercial, financial and banking activities.
	Capital requirements	A minimum of 50% of local capital (not less than L£3m) must remain in Lebanon.
	Interest payments and deposits	A tax of 10% is levied on interest payable on all deposits except savings accounts.
	Employment regulations	Foreigners must hold work permits.
Malaysia	New branches	The establishment of new foreign banks is not permitted, although representative offices are approved.
Mexico	New branches	Foreign banks are not permitted to acquire new holdings in domestic banks, although existing holdings may be retained.
Nigeria	New branches	Local incorporation of existing and new branches is mandatory. Certain finance activities are not open to foreign banks.
	Asset portfolio controls	40% of the total advances must be extended to domestic residents.
	Repatriation of profits	An exchange control premium is required on all funds transferred abroad.
	Employment regulations	Foreigners must hold work permits, subject to a quota.
Philippines	New branches	A licence is required for the establishment of new branches and representative offices which can be obtained from the Securities Exchange Commission.

Country	Area	Restrictions
Philippines *continued*	Capital requirements	In addition to the capital required of the domestic banks, 20% of the authorised capital must be subscribed, of which 25% must be held in cash or real estate.
	Repatriation of profits	Repatriation of profits is permitted in the currency of the original investment at the current exchange rate.
	Employment regulations	Foreigners must hold work permits.
Singapore	Capital requirements	Foreign banks are required to hold issued and paid-up capital of at least S$6m after deductions in respect of a debit balance, if any, appearing in the profit-and-loss account of the bank. The net head-office funds required for operations in Singapore must be not less than S$3m to be held as assets approved by the Commissioner of Banking.
	Employment regulations	Foreigners must hold work permits, subject to a quota of three foreign personnel per concern.
South Korea	New branches	Authorization for the establishment of new branches is required by the Monetary Board. Foreign enterprises are protected from expropriation by statute.
	Asset portfolio controls	Securities having maturities over 3 years cannot be held with the exception of national bonds and a minimum holding of 25% of Bank of Korea bonds. Foreign banks are permitted to own their banking premises, but no other real estate. The holding of capital or surpluses of any enterprise is limited to 10%. In the event of closure, Korean nationals receive priority in the distribution of assets.
	Repatriation of profits	Permission to remit profits must be obtained from the Minister of Finance.

Country	Area	Restrictions
Tanzania	New branches	New branches are not permitted. All commercial banks were taken over by the government-owned National Bank of Commerce.
	Repatriation of profits	Repatriation of profits is prohibited.
	Employment regulations	Nationals must be employed by foreign concerns, subject to qualification and availability.
Thailand	New branches	New banks cannot be established. The maximum equity holding permitted in existing banks by foreign investors is 40%.
	Repatriation of profits	Profits are subject to Thai taxation, with the exception of industries approved under the Industrial Investment Act, 1962, whose profits may be exempt from taxation for a period up to 5 years.
Uganda	New branches	New branches must be domestically incorporated with the permission of the Finance Minister.
	Employment regulations	Foreigners are required to hold work permits which are difficult to obtain.
Venezuela	New branches	The establishment of new branches is limited to those banks having a majority of Venezuelan-owned capital. Existing foreign-owned banks not reducing foreign participation to 20% are subject to restriction of banking activities. ·The establishment of representative offices is permitted.
	Capital requirements	Banks opening branches abroad or holding equity in foreign banks are required to hold a minimum of 40m bolivars.
	Employment regulations	A minimum of 75% of the labour employed must be nationals.
Zaire	Employment regulations	A quota on skilled foreign personnel is intended to encourage the employment of nationals.

Country	Area	Restrictions
Zambia	New branches	New foreign retail commercial banks are required to hold a licence. This authorization is given preferentially to banks having the majority of equity shares held by the government and Zambian nationals.
	Repatriation of profits	Up to 30% of equity capital may be transferred abroad, provided that the amount is less than 50% of net profits.

DIRECT INVESTMENT: OECD Countries

Country	Area	Restrictions
Austria	Minority ownership	Direct investment by non-residents is generally permitted if denominated in convertible currencies or from balances on free (originally owned), blocked or interim schilling accounts.
	Repatriation of profits	The transfer abroad of the following is permitted by the central bank: (i) proceeds from the liquidation of various foreign investments in Austria, such as shares or participation in domestic enterprises, securities or real estate; (ii) repayments by residents of foreign loans or credits.
Australia	Minority ownership	All enterprises in which more than 25% of the equity is held directly or indirectly by overseas interests are required to consult the central bank in respect of proposals to borrow in Australia. Acquisition by foreigners of 15% of the voting capital of a company is regarded as a foreign takeover. Measures exist for government control in such cases if they are contrary to the national interest.
	Repatriation of profits	All transfers of capital require approval of the central bank with no advance commitment given. Funds invested in securities quoted on the Australian Stock Exchange by

Country	Area	Restrictions
Australia— *continued*		residents of countries outside the Sterling Area can be repatriated in foreign currency at the official market rate.
Belgium-Luxembourg	Repatriation of profits	Exchange control authorities may guarantee the repatriation of approved foreign investments, which are allowed through the official market, subject to licence.
Canada	Minority ownership	Any group proposing a take-over of any existing domestic-owned company must notify the Foreign Investment Review Agency in writing. This applies to businesses having gross assets of over C$250,000 or a gross revenue of over C$3m. Every federally-chartered corporation must have a majority of Canadian directors. The foreign corporation must have a majority of those Canadian directors not maintaining an affiliation with that corporation in Canada or elsewhere.
	Repatriation of profits	A 15% withholding tax is levied on all transfers to non-residents, including Canadians residing outside of Canada.
Denmark	Minority ownership	Direct investment by non-residents does not require a special licence if the transaction concerns industry, commerce, handicrafts, hotel business or transportation. Other investments must be approved by the Ministry of Commerce.
France	Minority ownership	Direct investments are defined as investments implying control of a company or enterprise with ownership exceeding 20% of the capital whose shares are quoted on the stock exchange. Both foreign and domestic direct investment abroad require prior declaration to the Minister of Economy

Country	Area	Restrictions
France— continued		and Finance (Special Transactions Controls). Investment transactions concerning EEC member-countries require declaration under exchange control regulations. Prior exchange control authorization is necessary for transactions involving capital movements.
Greece	Repatriation of profits	Profits may be transferred abroad only if the investment is approved under the Foreign Investment Law.
Japan	Minority ownership	Up to 100% foreign ownership is permitted in newly established firms in specific fields, with 50% ownership permitted outside those fields. A small number of industries remain subject to a case-by-case screening. Aggregate foreign investment in existing firms is limited to 25% or 15% in certain industries.
Norway	Minority ownership	Foreign ownership of share capital exceeding 20% requires a concession from the Ministry of Industry.
Portugal	Minority ownership	Foreign investment by OECD, EFTA, IMF or IBRD member-country residents is encouraged in areas of recognized national interest, provided no speculative operation in real estate is involved. Investment in defence, public utilities, oil refining and fishing is restricted to firms having a majority of domestic capital. Prior authorization is required for both foreign and domestic investment in specific industries.
	Repatriation of profits	The transfer abroad of the full proceeds from the liquidation of foreign investment originating in a *bona fide* inward capital movement from OECD, EFTA, IMF or IBRD

Country	Area	Restrictions
Portugal— *continued*		member-countries is not restricted. Repatriation of profits exceeding 100,000 escudos requires authorization by the central bank, as does repatriation of funds.
Sweden	Minority ownership	Authorization is necessary for foreign direct investment, the transfer of liquidation proceeds (including appreciation) and real estate investment.
Turkey	Minority ownership	Foreign direct investment requires approval. Foreign firms must import capital in the form of foreign exchange, although in some cases blocked funds may be used for investment in the tourist industry. Certain investments must fall within the provisions of the Law for the Encouragement of Foreign Investments and the Petroleum Law. Borrowing funds in Turkish liras by foreign firms is subject to quotas set by the Ministry of Finance according to the firm's equity capital existing in Turkey.
	Repatriation of profits	Foreign capital invested in Turkey under the terms of the Law for the Encouragement of Foreign Investments is given preferential treatment provided that the proposed investment contributes to the economic development of Turkey or will operate in a field open to private domestic enterprises without entailing monopoly or requiring special privileges. Investments qualifying under this law are allowed to remit abroad all or part of the invested capital or foreign loans in the currency of the original investment.
United Kingdom	Minority ownership	Investment in the UK by non-residents must be approved by the Bank of England if it is to result in

Country	Area	Restrictions
United Kingdom— *continued*		ownership or control by non-residents. Although there are few restrictions on foreign investment in the UK, sources of finance to foreign-owned companies are blocked. Banks and other sources of finance in the UK must obtain permission to lend money or securities to companies owned or controlled by non-residents, as only working capital requirements may be met with sterling finance. Finance for the purchase of fixed assets is granted only to companies whose operations are regarded as being of "substantial benefit" to the UK economy, or are located in "development areas". Other foreign-owned companies are obliged to seek finance outside the sterling area and may only accept loans which are to be maintained for a period of at least five years.

DIRECT INVESTMENT: Developing Countries

Country	Area	Restrictions
Algeria	Repatriation of profits	A percentage of profits ranging to a maximum of 15% of the capital investment per annum can be transferred abroad. The percentage is determined by the size of the firm, the investment and the profits, although no fixed policy exists.
	Employment regulations	The employment of nationals is encouraged, although skilled foreign personnel are permitted.
Argentina	Minority ownership	New foreign investments require government approval under the Foreign Investments Law. Approval is preferentially given to those designed to improve the output of the export sector, to provide substitutes for imports and to improve existing technology.

Country	Area	Restrictions
Argentina— *continued*		Borrowing funds from domestic banks is permitted only for the purpose of export financing.
	Repatriation of profits	Repatriation of profits has been 'temporarily' suspended.
Bolivia	Minority ownership	Strategic industries such as metallurgy, chemicals and steel, are state-owned, although foreign investment participation is permitted.
	Repatriation of profits	Profits may be remitted abroad provided that the central bank has been previously informed of the operation.
	Favourable concessions	Special concessions are offered to encourage both foreign and domestic investors, such as exemptions from various taxes and customs duties, accelerated depreciation and tariff protection.
Brazil	Minority ownership	Foreign holdings are not permitted in publishing, shipping, fishing, oil, railways, television and radio stations. Companies with more than 5% foreign holdings are not permitted to renew contracts dependent on public concessions such as telephone and telegraph services, and the production and distribution of hydrocarbons and petroleum.
	Repatriation of profits	The remittance of profits on capital employed in the production of 'luxury items' is limited to 8% of registered capital per annum. Branch offices registered in Brazil having 50% or more voting capital held by its foreign parent-firm are prohibited from transferring profits or royalties abroad.
	Employment regulations	A minimum of two-thirds of the labour employed must be nationals.
	Repatriation of oil company earnings	Repatriation of oil company earnings is prohibited.

Country	Area	Restrictions
Colombia	Minority ownership	All new foreign direct investment projects must obtain approval. This authorization is preferentially given to projects whose net effect is to improve the balance of payments, employment and utilization of local raw materials.
	Repatriation of profits	Repatriation of profits is permitted to a maximum of 14% of the net value, in foreign currency, of the original investment. If the full 14% is not remitted in any one year the difference may be spread over the following periods, up to an additional 3% per annum.
Cyprus	Minority ownership	All foreign investment requires approval. Consideration is given to the purpose of the investment, the extent of possible foreign exchange earnings, the number of persons employed, the extent of the foreign exchange liability, and the probable competition with existing industries. Investments not exceeding 49% of the total share capital of a company are generally approved.
	Repatriation of profits	Profits, dividends and interest may be transferred abroad, after payment of any necessary charges and taxes and having Exchange Control approval.
Ghana	Minority ownership	Foreign investment requires prior approval by the Ministry of Finance and Economic Planning. The Capital Investment Act grants special benefits to specific existing investments as well as to new investments. Approval may be granted to investments that contribute to the development and utilization of productive capacity, the reduction of imports, the improvement of the level of employment or the increase of technical abilities of nationals.

Country	Area	Restrictions
Ghana— *continued*		Certain retail, wholesale and transportation operations are not open to foreign investments.
	Repatriation of profits	Investments approved under the Capital Investment Act may transfer 40–50% of the net profits and capital proceeds in the event of sale or liquidation.
		Profits of firms financed with domestic capital, owned by foreigners or owned/controlled by non-residents cannot be remitted abroad.
		Repatriation of the earnings of oil companies is not permitted.
	Favourable concessions	Tax holidays, initial capital allowances, etc. are available to investment projects approved under the Capital Investment Act.
Indonesia	Minority ownership	The Foreign Capital Investment Law permits foreign investment within specified industries, such as harbours, electric power, shipping, railroads, and commerce, only as a joint venture with a national. Firms that are wholly or largely operated in Indonesia must be incorporated locally. The operation permit for foreign investment is generally valid for a maximum of 30 years.
		Investment priorities are assigned to certain fields, with less consideration given to investments outside Java.
		Investments which generate saving of foreign exchange and improve the infrastructure are encouraged.
	Favourable concessions	Incentives for foreign investment include exemption from or reduction in corporate and dividend taxes for a certain period. Joint ventures with nationals may benefit from similar tax incentives. Other inducements include exemption from customs duties, accelerated depreciation allowances and permission to offset initial losses against subsequent profits.

Country	Area	Restrictions
Indonesia—*continued*		Foreign investments with a minimum capital of US$15m receive additional benefits.
Kenya	Repatriation od profits	To ensure the eventual repatriation of funds, a 'certificate of approved enterprise' must be obtained for the investment from the Treasury. A withholding tax of 12½% is levied on profits.
	Minority ownership	Foreign and domestic investment in specified types of production requires approval under the East African Licensing Ordinance.
Lebanon	Employment regulations	Foreigners must hold work permits.
Mexico	Minority ownership	Foreign investment is prohibited in electricity generation, insurance, finance and banking. Existing investment in banking and insurance can be maintained. Restrictions to investment of foreign funds exist in communications, transport services, fishing, food packaging, soft drinks, rubber, fertilizer, mining, chemical and agriculture.
	Employment regulations	A limited number of work permits are issued to foreigners.
Nigeria	Minority ownership	All foreign-owned firms and commercial banks that are operating locally must be incorporated locally. Direct investments must receive 'approved status' from the Ministry of Finance, which ensures consideration for repatriation of capital. The purchase of shares on the stock exchange is not permitted unless included in the original investment request.
	Repatriation of profits	The repatriation of foreign capital requires the approval of the Ministry of Finance.

Country	Area	Restrictions
Philippines	Minority ownership	Foreign direct investment and new foreign borrowing receive preferential treatment if approved by the Board of Investments (BOI), especially projects in export-oriented industries or those not requiring domestic credit facilities.
	Repatriation of profits	There are restrictions on the sale of foreign exchange for the repatriation of foreign direct investments, depending on the category of industry. Investments in BOI-approved industries and in non-export oriented industries not utilizing domestic credit facilities may be repatriated in five equal annual instalments commencing two years after the start of production.
	Employment regulations	Foreigners must hold a work permit which is non-renewable following a five-year period of employment. Foreigners may be employed in a supervisory, technical or advisory position, provided they do not exceed 5% of the total employed in each category. Nationals must be trained to replace the foreign employees following the five-year period.
	Repatriation of oil company earnings	Repatriation of the earnings of oil companies is prohibited.
Singapore	Minority earnings	New investments for 'pioneer' projects are granted approval if the existing industry is not able to meet the needs of the country. Specific incentives are offered under such conditions.
	Repatriation of profits	Repatriation is permitted subject to the approval of the foreign exchange authorities. Remittance of proceeds from the sale of capital assets is granted on a case-by-case basis.
	Employment regulations	A UK national is required to hold a valid re-entry permit, an employment pass, or a professional visitor's pass.

Country	Area	Restrictions
Singapore— continued		Foreigners earning less than S$750 per month also must hold a work permit.
South Korea	Minority ownership	In basic industries, foreign ownership exceeding 50% is not permitted.
Tanzania	Minority ownership	50% of any foreign investment project must be held by the government.
	Repatriation of profits	Repatriation of profits is permitted on the net profits accrued from foreign assets, the net proceeds of the sale of the enterprise, either in liquidation or as a going concern, the principal and interest of any foreign loan and up to one-third of expatriate gross earnings, subject to prior approval or the granting ot 'Foreign Investment Protection'.
	Employment regulations	Foreign firms must employ qualified nationals when available.
Trinidad and Tobago	Minority ownership	Foreign investors must hold a licence under the Aliens (Landholding) Ordinance in order to hold interest in real estate or shares in local companies.
	Favourable concessions	Certain concessions are granted to 'pioneer industries', which were not previously in existence or which are not presently being conducted on a commercial scale, or for which there are favourable prospects for future development. All 'pioneer' manufacturers are entitled to temporary relief from import duties and taxes, as well as other privileges.
Uganda	Minority ownership	To secure the guarantee of repatriation of funds, an investment must obtain an 'approved status' under the Foreign Investments (Protection) Act. Investments in specific industries require approval under the East African Industrial Licensing Act.

Country	Area	Restrictions
Uganda— *continued*	Repatriation of profits	Dividends and profits resulting from approved status investments are transferable according to the conditions of the approval.
	Employment regulations	Foreign firms are required to employ nationals.
Venezuela	Minority Ownership	Foreign investment in insurance companies is restricted to 40%, in banks to 20%, and in finance companies to 49%. No foreign investment is permitted in the exploitation of natural gas.
	Employment regulations	At least 75% of those employed must be nationals.
Zambia	Repatriation of profits	Up to 30% of equity capital can be remitted if the sum is less than 50% of net profits.

INSURANCE

Nationalization

Country	Particulars	Compensation
Burma	With effect from 1 February 1964, the Union Insurance Board was alone empowered to underwrite new general insurance business. The companies were given until 31 January 1965 to wind up existing business.	None.
Ceylon	Life assurance business was nationalized in 1966.	None.
	As from 1 January 1964, the Ceylon Insurance Corporation became the sole insurer in the country for non-life business.	None.
Dahomey	Nationalization of insurance was announced in December 1974 and state-run company established.	No information.

Country	Particulars	Compensation
Ethiopia	The Military Government announced its intention to nationalize insurance companies in December 1974.	Position awaits clarification.
India	Life assurance business was nationalized in 1956 and compensation was paid. As from 1 January 1973, the Central Government acquired the shares of all Indian non-life insurance companies and took control of foreign insurers. The General Insurance Corporation was set up to control the business with the day-to-day underwriting in the hands of four regional subsidiary companies.	Yes. The Nationalization Act provided for payment of "acquisition amounts" on an undisclosed basis. These amounts were considered by foreign insurers to be totally inadequate.
Pakistan	Life business of domestic and foreign companies was nationalized in March 1972 and from that date all life business was transferred to the State Life Insurance Corporation.	Under negotiation.
Syria	Within five years from 3 September 1959, all insurance companies operating in Syria were required to be of Arab nationality. Shareholders and directors must also be Arabs.	None.
Tanzania	From 1 January 1968, only the National Insurance Corporation was allowed to carry on general insurance business.	None.
Zambia	The Zambia State Insurance Corporation was given the sole right to carry on general business from 1 January 1972.	Claim lodged.

Appendix 1

Domestication

Country	Particulars
Dominican Republic	Law 126, which was effective from 20 August 1971, requires at least 51% of the capital of a company to be owned by Dominican citizens. This does not, however, apply to companies which had been operating for two years prior to the Law.
Ghana	The Insurance (Amendment) Decree 1972 required all insurance companies to be incorporated in Ghana and to have at least 40% of their shares in Ghanaian ownership.
Nigeria	The Companies Decree 1968 required all foreign companies to incorporate in Nigeria as separate entities from the parent company. The government is in process of acquiring a substantial minority shareholding in all foreign-owned insurance companies.
Peru	Decree Law 20088 requires all insurance companies to have more than 80% of capital owned by Peruvian nationals. Direct operations by foreign entities are not allowed.
Philippines	Presidential Decree 63 stated that from 20 November 1972, foreign companies may not invest more than an amount equal to 15% of their capital in any company in the Philippines and this investment must not exceed 20% of the capital of the Philippines company. A revised Insurance Code has just been signed by the President, details of its provisions are awaited.
Spain	Foreign participation in the capital of Spanish insurance companies is limited to 50%.
Uganda	The Finance Act 1970 laid down that insurance business may only be transacted by a company incorporated in the country. The Companies (Government & Public Bodies) Act 1970 provides for the Government to acquire 60% of the share holding of any locally incorporated company.
Venezuela	All insurance companies are expected to have at least 50% of their capital held by Venezuelans and a Venezuelan majority on their boards.

Prohibitions on Insurance Abroad

Country	Restrictions
Brazil	The Law regulating the transaction of insurance in Brazil limits the placing of insurance and reinsurance abroad to risks that cannot be covered in the country, and whenever this placing occurs it has to be effected through the National Reinsurance Institute (I.R.B.).
Columbia	It is prohibited to insure with companies not registered in Colombia. If an insured takes out a policy with an unauthorised insurer then he incurs a penalty of 50% of the premium unless the Supervisory Department authorises such insurance on the grounds that no companies in Colombia are prepared to accept the business.
Italy	The insurance abroad of ships and aircraft requires the authorization of the Ministry of Industry.
Portugal	Portuguese law forbids any insurance to be taken out by or on behalf of any person with any concern not licensed to undertake insurance in Portugal. As a consequence, insurance may be taken out only with duly licensed Portuguese concerns or branches/agencies of foreign concerns.
	Where Portuguese concerns or branches of foreign concerns will not accept particular risks or will accept only at rates of premium deemed to be excessive, the insurance may with the permission of the Inspectorate General of Credit and Insurance by placed abroad.
Switzerland	While Swiss legislation forbids an unlicensed insurer from effecting insurances in Switzerland with residents of Switzerland it does not affect in principle a person's freedom to take out insurance or to choose his insurer. However, a person may not take out abroad
	(a) any insurance for which a monopoly has been granted, or
	(b) any compulsory insurance where the law affects the choice of insurer and requires the insurer to be licensed in Switzerland.
	(Throughout the Federation the Caisse Nationale Suisse d'Assurance has a monopoly of compulsory insurance against occupational injury and diseases. Seven cantons have instituted compulsory sickness insurance which has

Country	Restrictions
Switzerland—*continued*	to be covered by especially constituted sickness funds, and a number have a monopoly of fire insurance covering buildings, furniture and personal effects.)
Venezuela	Policies covering risks located in Venezuela and insured abroad are not legally enforceable in Venezuela unless the premium is paid in Venezuela to a registered insurer and the rates conform to those approved by the Venezuelan authorities.

Restrictions on Remittances

Country	Restrictions
Dominican Republic	In February 1972 the government issued a Resolution imposing a limit on the amount of profits which can be re-submitted abroad. This is 18% of the net value of investment, but relates only to certain listed fields of operation which do not include insurance. However, those persons or entities falling outside those listed are entitled to remit up to 18% of the net value of the investment, provided that such investments were registered with the Central Bank at the time of the Resolution. Remittances in respect of reinsurance premiums are in theory allowed, subject to "satisfactory identification" of the funds concerned. In practice, the formalities involved in satisfying the authorities have been used by them in some cases to prevent remittances being made.
Ghana	Restrictions are reportedly due to shortage of foreign exchange. The position has eased somewhat from former levels of restriction.
Tunisia	Although only two groups of companies currently operate, several have withdrawn over the last decade and all of these companies have been unable to secure remittance since 1960 of bank balances and, in the case of the companies which have withdrawn, deposits and surplus assets, even though their liabilities have ceased.

Localization of Funds

Country	Particulars	Requirements
Barbados	The Act requires the setting up of deposits for general insurance business to the extent of 40% of the premium income, (non-life classes) with a maximum of EC$ 200,000.	In prescribed securities, including government bonds (of Barbados Government and other Commonwealth governments, although the latter is restricted to a maximum of 10% of the required deposit), debentures, mortgages, real estate and freehold.
Pakistan	Under the 1938 Insurance Act as amended general insurers are required to lodge the following deposits with the State Bank of Pakistan:	Cash.

Fire Rs. 150,000　Rs. 150,000
Marine　　　　　Rs. 150,000
Miscellaneous　　Rs. 150,000
Any two classes　Rs. 250,000
All three classes　Rs. 350,000

Furthermore, all companies must have invested in Pakistan in respect of their Pakistan business assets exceeding liabilities by Rs. 500,000 or 10% of their Pakistan premium income, whichever is the greater.

| Philippines | By Presidential Decree the Insurance Act has been amended to provide that foreign insurance companies must deposit with the Insurance Commission an amount not less than the capital of domestic insurance companies. This is at present an amount of Pesos 2 m. | In Philippines securities. |

Country	Particulars	Requirements
Philippines—continued	It is also provided that foreign companies must retain in the Philippines assets which are in excess of their total liabilities (a trusted surplus) by an amount equivalent to the deposit.	50% in Philippines securities and 50% securities acceptable to the Commission.
St Lucia	Under an amendment to the Insurance Act dated December 1974 the maximum guarantee deposit required of a foreign company (which has to be invested in St Lucian security) is $100,000 against a figure of $50,000 for local companies.	
St Vincent	The Insurance Act of 1971 requires the following deposits: Long-term business WI$ 50,000 Motor business WI$ 50,000 or 30% of premium income, whichever is the greater Other business WI$ 15,000 The Minister has power to waive or modify the requirement to the extent of any certificate as to assets provided by the insurer's own country.	
Trinidad	Deposits are required as follows: Long term business TT$ 250,000 (except in the case of domestic companies, which are required to have capital in that amount) Motor business TT$ 250,000 or 40% of the year's premium whichever is the greater One or more other classes TT$ 100,000 or 40% of the year's premium whichever is the greater. There are also requirements for	Approved securities are specified as follows: (a) Trinidad and Tobago government stocks in TT$ (b) Up to 30% Trinidad and Tobago stocks in other currency. (c) Any other Commonwealth government up to a limit of 10% (d) The US

Country	Particulars	Requirements
Trinidad— *continued*	statutory funds* for long-term and motor business, i.e. 80% of net unearned premiums *pro rata* per month, plus outstanding losses less (in the case of motor business) the deposit.	government or any other approved country – limit 10% *Statutory Fund Approved Securities: motor business: 60% minimum in local currency assets + 40% maximum in UK and Common-wealth government issues (long-term requirements not known).

Compulsory Cessions

Country	Particulars
Argentina	Law 12988 of 1947 established the State Reinsurance Corporation, originally known as IMAR which was subsequently changed to INDER in Argentina with a capital of $12 m contributed equally by the Argentine State and the Argentine insurance companies. The Law requires all national companies to cede the excess of their retentions to INDER in all classes and foreign companies to make a compulsory cession of not less than 30% in respect of fire and motor business.

Furthermore, the foreign companies receive commission terms which do not cover their acquisition costs and which were less favourable than those paid to the national companies. Representations regarding this have been made on several occasions.

Early in 1973, INDER announced Resolution 4556 requiring the compulsory cessions for foreign companies to be increased from 30% to 60%, but the same commission as for national companies will be paid on the additional 30% cession.

Following representations made by the embassies of the foreign companies represented in Argentina and the Association of Foreign Insurers, INDER proposed that as an alternative the compulsory 30% cession should remain, but the foreign companies would be obliged to

Country	*Particulars*

Argentina—
continued

cede the excess of their own retention at the same commission rates granted to Argentine companies, with no restriction on the level of limits. A few foreign companies have taken up this alternative and arrangements have been put in hand for the relevant treaty to be drawn up with INDER for the ceding of the 30% compulsory cession and the excess of the companies' retention.

A further Resolution, number 4569, has been published by INDER requiring foreign companies to make compulsory cessions in respect of various classes of accident business on the same lines as outlined above.

Brazil

The Reinsurance Institute of Brazil (IRB) was created by Decree Law No. 1186 of 1939 to control reinsurance and retrocession operations in Brazil.

The initial share capital was fixed at Cr. $42 m divided equally between domestic insurance companies created by Federal Law and joint stock companies and mutuals authorised to transact insurance.

Companies' retentions are fixed by a formula laid down by the Superintendent of Insurance which is varied each year, and companies are obliged to cede the excess of their retention to the IRB.

Commissions for fire business range from 22% to 28% depending on the loss ratio for the previous year. This does not cover their acquisition costs. As regards the other classes, the commission terms are comparable to normal acquisition costs.

Chile

The Reinsurance Bank of Chile (Caja Reaseguradora de Chile) was established by Law No. 4228 of 1927. The original share capital of the company was Esc. 15 m divided equally between the State, the companies and individuals. However, as a result of legislation requiring the insurance companies to invest 5% of their capital and reserves in the shares of the Reinsurance Bank, they now have a majority shareholding.

Foreign companies are obliged to cede 20% of all policies to the Caja, but at very low commission rates, which are approximately 60% of normal acquisition commission. The current rate of commission in respect of fire business ammounts to 28.0575%.

Country	Particulars

Nigeria

The National Insurance Corporation of Nigeria (NICON) was established on 1 July 1969 to carry on any class of insurance business, including life.

The share capital is £1 m, all the shares being owned by the Nigerian Government, and is fully paid up. As from 1 October 1969, every registered insurer was made liable to cede 10% of its business to the Corporation, which reserves the right to refuse any business at its discretion.

The government has power, by order, to alter the rate of cession or the classes of business to be so subject.

In implementation of the Act, insurers were obliged from 1 October 1969 to cede 10% of accident business, excluding certain categories such as public liability, engineering, performance bonds, etc. and contractors' all risks. Rates of commission (profit commission forbidden by law) were originally the subject of representations to the Corporation, and some have been very marginally increased. The rates are now:

Motor	25%
Workmen's compensation	17.5%
Other accident	25%

As from 1 January 1971, it became necessary to cede 10% of all fire business, the rate of commission being 30%, and with effect from 1 July 1974, NICON extended the 10% compulsory concessions to include public liability, contractors' all risks and engineering insurances.

Pakistan

The Pakistan Insurance Corporation was founded in 1952, the government having a majority shareholding. Government control is exerted also by the appointment of the managing director, chairman and government directors, who are in a majority and dictate the policies of the Corporation.

Insurance companies are legally required to make cessions to the Corporation, subject to a maximum of 30% all classes − 50% of this is ceded back. An Act passed in 1967, but not yet enforced, required insurers to reinsure with the Corporation all surpluses beyond their net retentions and the compulsory cession and local reinsurance ceded.

Rates of commission are fixed periodically, but unlike some other areas, are generally in line with market conditions.

Public Procurement

Country	Particulars
Argentina	1. Any firm or individual in Argentina who enjoys any of a wide variety of vaguely defined concessions, franchises, tax abatements, etc. must insure their interests exclusively with Argentine insurance companies. 2. All government, provincial, municipal and other official insurance interests must be placed with Argentine companies. 3. Only Argentine companies may insure imports into Argentina which are for the account of the importer. 4. The commission paid to foreign companies on the first 30% of the compulsory cessions to INDER (the State Reinsurance Entity) is restricted to the original acquisition commission cost without any reimbursement of other acquisition costs, whereas domestic companies receive a much higher rate of commission.
Ghana	Insurances effected by government, statutory corporations or any bodies in which government or a statutory corporation owns more than 50% of the proprietary interest and insurances effected in respect of any property or interest held by or in trust for the government, a statutory corporation or any such bodies must all be placed with the Ghana State Insurance Corporation.
Kenya	All government insurances including statutory boards, local authorities and cooperatives are directed to the Kenya National Assurance Company.
Switzerland	In certain parts of the country, fire insurance on buildings is compulsory and has to be placed compulsorily with the cantonal insurance companies.

Employment of Expatriates

Country	Particulars
France	A resident permit and a work permit must be obtained from the Ministry of Employment and the employer must be able to show that the vacancy cannot be readily filled by a national.
Mexico	Only a limited number of work permits are made available.

Country	Particulars
Venezuela	At least 75 per cent of those employed must be nationals.

SHIPPING: OECD Countries

Country	Area	Restrictions
Australia	Coastal trade	Foreign vessels must be licensed. Provision for issue of permits to unlicenced carriers when licence is not available.
	Unilateral reservation of cargo	40% of all goods must be carried in Australian bottoms.
Canada	Coastal trade	Foreign participation is restricted in all waters west of Havre St Pierre (north shore) and Cape des Rosiers (south shore) on the St Lawrence River.
Denmark	Coastal trade	Freighters under 500 tons gross require a special licence.
France	Coastal trade	Foreign participation is not permitted, including trade between Martinique, Guadaloupe and Guyana.
	Unilateral reservation of cargo	Exclusive transport rights for all national defence goods, 40% of coal tonnage, two-thirds of petroleum tonnage and exclusive transport of bananas are held by national flag vessels.
	Bilateral reservation of cargo	Monopoly traffic between metropolitan France and Tunisia and Algeria is given to national flag vessels.
Germany	Coastal trade	Foreign participation is permitted only when national flag vessels are not available or are exceeding quoted costs of foreign vessels.
	Unilateral reservation of cargo	Foreign aid cargoes must be transported by national flag vessels.

Country	Area	Restrictions
Greece	Coastal trade Bilateral agreements on cargo	Foreign participation is prohibited. Agreements have been signed with member countries of the Geneva Convention, 1923. Non-member vessels pay an additional charge of 100%
Japan	Coastal trade	Foreign participation is not permitted.
Luxembourg	Coastal trade	Foreign participation is not permitted.
New Zealand	Bilateral agreements on cargo	Cargo regulations are set by British conference lines agreements.
Norway	Fiscal subsidies	Subsidization for maintenance of remote services.
Turkey	Coastal trade	Foreign participation is not permitted.
	Unilateral reservations of cargo	A slight preference is given to Red Flag vessels.
United States	Coastal trade	Cabotage trade is permitted only when national flag vessels are not available or under special circumstances, subject to the permission of the Federal Maritime Commission.
	Unilateral reservation of cargo	Defence supplies are to be carried only by national flag vessels, as are agricultural products financed by the government. 50% of USAID cargo and goods covered by the EX-IM Bank Loan must be transported by national flag vessels.
	Fiscal subsidies	Subsidies are given to protect the domestic shipbuilding and related operations on wages and repairs, etc. Lines accepting subsidization are required to make a specified number of calls at certain ports on certain routes.
	Other barriers	The US Revenue Act established Domestic International Sales Corpora-

Country	Area	Restrictions
United States— continued		tions (DISCs). A company receives tax deferment along with reduction in freight and other costs if it qualifies as an active exporter using at least 50% of national flag bottoms.

SHIPPING: Developing Countries

Country	Area	Restrictions
Algeria	Coastal trade	Foreign participation is not permitted.
Argentina	Coastal trade	Foreign participation is not permitted.
	Unilateral reservation of cargo	Government and private purchases and sales of goods as well as government-financed imports are reserved for national flag vessels, unless exemption is authorized by the Director of the Merchant Marine. Conference freight rates must be registered and approved by the Secretary of State for Transport.
	Bilateral agreements on cargo reservation	Equal access agreements operate with Brazil, Chile, Colombia, Lebanon, Peru, Venezuela and the USSR. Two US lines have permission to cover the southbound movement of government-controlled cargo.
	Other barriers	Regulations that favour national flag vessels include reduced port charges, rebates on wharfage fees on a tonnage basis, as well as the elimination of consular fees. Export credit may be up to 85% of freight if transported under the national flag. 50% of US (A.10) shipments are reserved for national flag vessels. Tax rebates for manufactured exports are calculated at f.o.b. value when shipped in foreign bottoms and at c.i.f. value when shipped in Argentine bottoms.

Country	Area	Restrictions
Bolivia	Coastal trade	Inland waterway transport is reserved for national flag ships when available. Foreign vessels require temporary authorization when no national flag vessel is available.
	Unilateral reservation of cargo	Between 30—50% of all cargo in trade is served by the national flag line. Government and official imports and exports are legally reserved for national flag ships when available.
	Bilateral agreements on cargo reservation	Preference is given to national flag ships under the Bolivian-Uruguay trade agreement.
Brazil	Coastal trade	Foreign participation is not permitted unless no national flag vessel is available.
	Unilateral reservation of cargo	Any imports purchased by public authorities such as the railways or petroleum industries, or bought with government assistance must be carried in national flag vessels. Only new Freight Conference members can carry liner cargo into Brazil.
		Exports and imports enjoying favourable treatment such as special tariff concessions, preferential internal fiscal treatment or preferential credit facilities, or are financed by national banks or by internationsl loans are subject to waiver in favour of foreign flag vessels under certain circumstances.
	Bilateral agreements on cargo reservation	50—50 cargo sharing agreements operate with Argentina, Chile, Portugal, Uruguay and Yugoslavia. Three US lines have sailing, pooling and equal access agreements with national flag lines.
		An agreement with the United States permits equal sharing of government—controlled cargoes in southbound trade. Third flag carriage is permitted only if neither US nor Brazilian flag vessels are available.

Country	Area	Restrictions
Brazil—*continued*	Fiscal subsidies	A stamp tax of 4.0 cruzeiros is levied on freight carried in foreign bottoms. A tax credit is granted on all Brazilian manufactured goods. Tax is calculated at f.o.b. value when carried in foreign bottoms and at c.i.f. value when carried in Brazilian bottoms.
	Other barriers	Brazilian flag vessels are exempt from lighthouse duties and receive reductions in pilotage fees of 40% at Santos and 30% at Rio de Janeiro.
Burma	Coastal trade	Foreign participation is not permitted.
	Unilateral reservation of cargo	All national flag lines are state-owned under control of a government trading organization which gives preferential treatment to national flag vessels.
Chile	Coastal trade	Foreign participation is not permitted unless no national flag vessel is available.
	Unilateral reservation of cargo	Cargoes of state enterprises and 50% of imports and exports must be carried in national flag bottoms. Government cargoes and government-owned enterprises' cargo or cargo in which Chile has an interest must be carried in national flag vessels or a Chilean-owned line. Import licences are required which act as a further barrier.
	Bilateral agreements on cargo reservation	Fifty-fifty sharing clauses are contained in agreements with Argentina, Brazil and the United States. An equal access agreement has been made with Peru.
	Other barriers	Freight dues are higher for those vessels not regularly serving Chilean ports.
Colombia	Coastal trade	Foreign participation is not permitted.
	Unilateral	Goods must be imported on a f.o.b.

Country	Area	Restrictions
Columbia—*continued*	reservation of cargo	value basis with foreign insurance paid in the Colombian currency. A minimum of 50% of cargo transported on established routes must use national flag vessels. A maximum of 50% of all bulk, liquid and refrigerated import and export goods must be carried in national flag bottoms.
	Bilateral agreements on cargo reservation	Agreements have been made with Argentina, Uruguay and the United States containing 50-50 sharing clauses on cargo. Equal access agreements have been made with the Colombian national line and two US lines.
Cyprus	Coastal trade	Foreign participation is not permitted.
Ecuador	Coastal trade	Foreign participation is not permitted.
	Unilateral reservation of cargo	All government and official imports 50% of crude oil and 20-30% of other cargo are to be carried on the National Merchant Fleets and national flag vessels. A minimum of 50% of all hydrocarbons imported to or exported from Ecuador must be carried by 'Transnave', a consortium of Japanese and Ecuadorean interests.
Ghana	Coastal trade	There are no restrictions on foreign participation in the insignificant coastal trade.
	Unilateral reservation of cargo	Import licences require imports to be carried on the state-owned Black Star Line. At least 25% of national timber is to be shipped in national flag bottoms.
India	Coastal trade	Foreign participation is not permitted.
	Unilateral reservation	EX—IM bulk cargoes not carried in US bottoms must be carried in

Country	Area	Restrictions
India— *continued*	of cargo	national flag bottoms. All bulk and general dry cargo may be carried in non-national flag vessels. Iron ore cargoes are encouraged to be carried by national flag vessels. The general policy is to buy at f.o.b. value and to sell at c.i.f. value.
	Bilateral agreements on cargo reservation	Agreements containing 50-50 clauses such as the India—United Arab Republic agreement and those containing 'best endeavours' clauses to allocate bilateral cargoes have been made with Iran, Poland, Rumania, the USSR, Czechoslovakia, Hungary, East Germany and Peru.
	Other barriers	Reductions in port charges have been made on national flag carriers of Iran.
Indonesia	Coastal trade Unilateral reservation of cargo	Foreign participation is not allowed. 45% of all cargo is to be shipped in national flag bottoms.
	Bilateral agreements on cargo reservation	Bilateral agreements with 50-50 sharing clauses have been made with Singapore and the USSR. The United Arab Republic agreement includes a 'best endeavours' clause to allocate bilateral cargoes.
Jordan	Coastal trade	Foreign participation is not permitted.
Lebanon	Coastal trade	No restriction on foreign participation.
	Unilateral reservation of cargo	The Lebanese Shipping Company has preference in cargoes transported to Lebanon, the Red Sea area, North African and other African countries. Cargo preference is considered in the licencing procedure for imports. A pledge is required insuring that cargoes will not be shipped on Israeli or other black-listed vessels.

Country	Area	Restrictions
Morocco	Coastal trade	Foreign participation is not permitted.
	Unilateral reservation of cargo	40% of imports and 30% of certain imported commodities must be shipped in national flag bottoms.
		Government and government-sponsored companies give preferential treatment to national flag vessels. Non-national vessels may be used only when national flag vessels are not available.
Pakistan	Coastal trade	Foreign participation is permitted only when national flag vessels are not available.
	Unilateral reservation of cargo	50% of US and World Bank aid cargoes are to be carried in national flag bottoms.
		Letters of credit favouring Pakistani bottoms as well as requiring freight payable at the destination in non-transferable currency discriminate in favour of national flag vessels.
	Bilateral agreements on cargo reservation	Bilateral agreements have been made with Egypt, India, Poland and the United Arab Republic.
Philippines	Coastal trade	Foreign participation is not permitted.
	Unilateral reservation of cargo	Exports and imports of goods that are consigned as government entities which are available after ten days time are to be transported by national flag vessels.
		Government-financed imports are to be carried in national flag bottoms.
		Communist flag vessels with the exception of Yugoslavia and Bulgaria are prohibited from carrying cargoes destined for or transported from the Philippines.
	Fiscal subsidies	The Investment Incentives Act, 1967, allows a deduction from taxable income in respect of ocean freight of

Country	Area	Restrictions
Philippines— *continued*		twice the amount paid on domestic exports, provided the carrier is in route to a regular port of call. A deduction of 150% is permitted by exporters on freight payments to non-national vessels transporting goods to a port not included in the normal route.
Singapore	Coastal trade	Foreign participation is not permitted.
	Bilateral agreements on cargo reservation	A bilateral agreement has been made with Indonesia.
South Korea	Coastal trade	Foreign participation is not permitted.
	Unilateral reservation of cargo	Preferential treatment toward national flag vessels is provided by government contracting on a c.i.f. value basis enabling national flag vessels to enjoy a more equal ground for competition. Non-national flag ships must be used only when national flag vessels are not available.
Tanzania	Coastal trade	No restriction on foreign participation.
Thailand	Coastal trade	Foreign participation is not permitted.
	Unilateral reservation of cargo	Government cargo is encouraged to be imported on a f.o.b. basis. Shipowners require a licence to transport certain cargo. Non-compliance is penalized.
Trinidad and Tobago	Coastal trade	No restriction on foreign participation.
United Arab Republic	Coastal trade	Foreign participation is not permitted.
	Unilateral reservation of cargo	30% of imports and exports are to be carried in national flag bottoms.
	Bilateral	Discriminatory clauses concerning

Country	Area	Restrictions
United Arab Republic—*continued*	agreements on cargo reservation	shipping are included in agreements with Ceylon, Indonesia, Libya, Pakistan, Rumania, the USSR, East Germany, Hungary and Yugoslavia.
Venezuela	Coastal trade	Foreign participation is not permitted.
	Unilateral reservation of cargo	Duty-free imports must be carried on national flag vessels. Imports are exempt from import duties when transported in national flag bottoms.

TRAVEL: OECD Countries

Country	Restrictions on own residents' overseas travel
Australia	An exchange allowance of A$100 in any twelve month period for travel in any country. Additional amounts may be obtained on application.
Canada	No more than C$5 in silver coins can be taken out of Canada.
Denmark	An allowance of 2,000 krone in bank notes and coins plus any amount denominated in foreign currency.
France	An exchange allocation for tourism of 1,500 francs per person for two separate trips per calendar year. An allowance for business travel of 400 francs per person per day subject to a maximum of 4,000 francs per trip.
Italy	An allowance of 1m lire per trip for tourism, business, medical treatment or education. Additional amounts can be obtained provided no unauthorized capital transfer occurs.
Japan	A tourist allowance equivalent to US$3,000 per person.
Norway	A tourist allowance of 350 krone per trip in bank notes and coins plus 5,000 krone per trip denominated in foreign currency.

TRAVEL: Developing Countries

Country	Restrictions on own residents' overseas travel
Algeria	A tourist allowance equivalent to £8 per person per annum.
Brazil	A tourist allowance of US$1,000 per person per trip. Additional amounts require the prior approval of the central bank.
Ghana	A tourist allowance of £50 per visit, with business allowances considered on merit.
Philippines	A tourist allowance of US$500 in foreign currency per annum for travel to Europe and the United States. The allowance for travel to Asia is US$250 per annum. Foreign exchange for business travel is dependent on the purpose, with export projects encouraged.
Singapore	Residents are allowed up to S$10,000 in foreign currency per person per annum.
South Korea	Residents are allowed K$100 in foreign exchange. Additional amounts may be obtained according to the purpose of the trip.
Tanzania	Residents are allowed Shs 4,000 per person in any three-year period.
Thailand	A travel allowance of 500 baht plus US$140 per person.
Trinidad and Tobago	A basic tourist allowance of TT$2,000 per annum with business and professional travel allowances of TT$100 per day for a maximum period of two months.
Uganda	A tourist allowance of £75 per person per annum. The business allowance permits £23 per person per day, with additional amounts permitted for travel in Canada and the United States.
Zaire	A tourist allowance of US$30 per person per day. The business allowance is at the discretion of the authorities.
Zambia	A tourist allowance of K600 per person in any two-year period.

Extracts from the OECD Code for the Liberalization of Capital Movements

Undertakings with Regard to Current Invisible Operations

Article 1: General Undertakings

(a) Members shall eliminate between one another, in accordance with the provisions of Article 2, restrictions on current invisible transactions and transfers, hereinafter called "current invisible operations". Measures designed for this purpose are hereinafter called "measures of liberalization".

(b) Where members are not bound, by virtue of the provisions of this Code, to grant authorization in respect of current invisible operations, they shall deal with applications in as liberal a manner as possible.

(c) Members shall use their best offices to ensure that the measures of liberalization are applied within their overseas territories.

(d) Members shall endeavour to extend the measures of liberalization to all members of the International Monetary Fund.

(e) "Member" shall mean a Member of the Organization which adheres to this Code.

Article 2: Measures of Liberalization

(a) Members shall grant any authorization required for a current invisible operation specified in an item set out in Annex A to this Code.

(b) A member may lodge reservations relating to the obligations resulting from paragraph (a) when:

(i) an item is added to Annex A to this Code;

(ii) obligations relating to an item in that Annex are extended; or

(iii) obligations relating to any such item being to apply to that member.

Reservations shall be set out in Annex B to this Code.

Article 3: Public Order and Security

The provisions of this Code shall not prevent a member from taking action which it considers necessary for:

(i) the maintenance of public order or the protection of public health, morals and safety;

(ii) the protection of its essential security interests; or

(iii) the fulfilment of its obligations relating to international peace and security.

Article 4: Obligations in Existing Multilateral International Agreements

Nothing in this Code shall be regarded as altering the obligations undertaken by a Member as a Signatory of the Articles of Agreement of the International Monetary Fund or other existing multilateral international agreements.

Article 5: Controls and Formalities

(a) The measures of liberalization provided for in this Code shall not limit the powers of members to verify the authenticity of current invisible operations nor to take any measures required to prevent evasion of their laws or regulations.

(b) Members shall simplify as much as possible all formalities connected with the authorization or verification of current invisible operations, and shall co-operate, if necessary, to attain such simplification.

Article 6: Execution of Transfers

(a) A member shall be deemed to have complied with its obligations as regards transfers whenever a transfer may be made:

(i) between persons entitled, by the exchange regulations of the State from which and of the State to which the transfer is to be made, respectively, to make and/or to receive the said transfer;

(ii) in accordance with international agreements in force at the time the transfer is to be made; and

(iii) in accordance with the monetary arrangements in force between the State from which and the State to which the transfer is to be made.

(b) The provisions of paragraph (a) do not preclude members from demanding payment of maritime freights in the currency of a third State, provided that such a demand is in conformity with established maritime practice.

Article 7: Clauses of Derogation

(a) If its economic and financial situation justifies such a course, a member need not take the whole of the measures of liberalization provided for in Article 2(a).

(b) If any measures of liberalization taken or maintained in accordance with the provisions of Article 2(a) result in serious economic disturbance in the Member State concerned, that member may withdraw those measures.

(c) If the overall balance of payments of a member develops adversely, at a rate and in circumstances, including the state of its monetary reserves, which it considers serious that member may temporarily suspend the application of measures of liberalization taken or maintained in accordance with the provisions of Article 2(a).

(d) However, a member invoking paragraph (c) shall endeavour to ensure that its measures of liberalization:

(i) cover, twelve months after it has invoked that paragraph, to a reasonable extent, having regard to the need for advancing towards the objective defined in subparagraph (ii), current invisible operations which the member must authorize in accordance with Article 2(a) and the authorization of which it has suspended since it invoked paragraph (c), and, in particular current invisible operations relating to tourism, if, in whole or in part, their authorization has been suspended; and

(ii) comply, eighteen months after it has invoked that paragraph, with its obligations under Article 2(a).

(e) Any member invoking the provisions of this Article shall do so in such a way as to avoid unnecessary damage which bears especially on the commercial or economic interests of another member and, in particular, shall avoid any discrimination between other members.

OECD Code of Liberalization of Current Invisible Operations

Part I   Undertakings with Regard to Capital Movements

Article 1: General Undertakings

(a) Members shall progressively abolish between one another, in accordance with the provisions of Article 2, restrictions on movements of capital to the extent necessary for effective economic co-operation. Measures designed to eliminate such restrictions are hereinafter called "measures of liberalization".

(b) Members shall, in particular, endeavour:

(i) to treat all non-resident owned assets in the same way irrespective of the date of their formation, and

(ii) to permit the liquidation of all non-resident owned assets and the transfer of such assets or of their liquidation proceeds.

(c) Members should use their best offices to ensure that the measures of liberalization are applied within their overseas territories.

(d) Members shall endeavour to extend the measures of liberalization to all members of the International Monetary Fund.

(e) Members shall endeavour to avoid introducing any new exchange restrictions on the movements of capital or the use of non-resident owned funds and shall endeavour to avoid making existing regulations more restrictive.

Article 2: Measures of Liberalization

(a) Subject to the provisions of paragraph (b) (iv), Members shall grant any authorization required for the conclusion or execution of transactions and for transfers specified in an item set out in List A or List B of Annex A to this Code.

(b) A Member may lodge reservations relating to the obligations resulting from paragraph (a) when:

(i) an item is added to List A of Annex A to this Code;

(ii) obligations relating to an item in that List are extended;

(iii) obligations relating to any such item begin to apply to that Member; or

(iv) at any time, in respect of an item in List B.

Reservations shall be set out in Annex B to the Code.

(c) Whenever the liquidation proceeds of non-resident owned assets may be transferred, the right of transfer shall include any appreciation of the original assets.

(d) Whenever existing regulations or international agreements permit loans between residents of different Members otherwise than by issuing marketable domestic securities or by using, in the country in which the borrower resides, funds the transfer of which is restricted, the repayment obligation may be expressed or guaranteed in the currency of either of the two Members concerned.

Article 3: Public Order and Security

The provisions of this Code shall not prevent a member from taking action which it considers necessary for:

(i) the maintenance of public order or the protection of public health morals and safety;

(ii) the protection of its essential security interests;

(iii) the fulfilment of its obligations relating to international peace and security.

Article 4: Obligations in Existing Multilateral International Agreements

Nothing in this Code shall be regarded as altering the obligations undertaken by a Member as a Signatory of the Articles of Agreement, of the International Monetary Fund or other existing multilateral international agreements.

Article 5: Controls and Formalities

(a) The measures of liberalization provided for in this Code shall not limit the powers of Members to verify the authenticity of transactions or transfers nor to take any measures required to prevent evasion of their laws or regulations.

(b) Members shall simplify as much as possible all formalities connected with the authorization or verification of transactions or transfers, and shall co-operate, if necessary, to attain such simplification.

Article 6: Execution of Transfers

A Member shall be deemed to have complied with its obligations as regards transfers whenever a transfer may be made:

(i) between persons entitled, by the exchange regulations of the State from which and of the State to which the transfer is to be made, respectively, to make and/or to receive the said transfer;

(ii) in accordance with international agreements in force at the time the transfer is to be made; and

(iii) in accordance with the monetary arrangements in force between the State from which and the State to which the transfer is to be made.

Article 7: Clauses of Derogation

(a) If its economic and financial situation justifies such a course, a Member need not take the whole of the measures of liberalization provided for in Article 2(a).

(b) If any measures of liberalization taken or maintained in accordance with the provisions of Article 2(a) result in serious economic and financial disturbance in the Member State concerned, that Member may withdraw those measures.

(c) If the overall balance of payments of a Member develops, adversely at a rate and in circumstances, including the state of its monetary reserves, which it considers serious, that Member may temporarily suspend the application of measures of liberalization taken or maintained in accordance with the provisions of Article 2(a).

(d) However, a Member invoking paragraph (c) shall endeavour to ensure that its measures of liberalization:

(i) cover, twelve months after it has invoked that paragraph, to a reasonable extent, having regard to the need for advancing towards the objective defined in subparagraph (ii), transactions and transfers which the Member must authorize in accordance with Article 2(a) and the authorization of which it has suspended, since it invoked paragraph (c); and

(ii) comply, eighteen months after it has invoked that paragraph, with its obligations under Article 2(a).

(c) Any Member invoking the provisions of this Article shall do so in such a way as to avoid unnecessary damage which bears especially on the financial or economic interests of another Member and, in particular, shall avoid any discrimination between other Members.

Article 8: Right to Benefit from Measures of Liberalization

Any Member lodging a reservation under Article 2(b) or invoking the provisions of Article 7 shall, nevertheless, benefit from the measures of liberalization taken by other Members, provided it has complied with the procedure laid down in Article 12 or Article 13 as the case may be.

Article 9: Non-Discrimination

A Member shall not discriminate as between other Members in authorizing the conclusion and execution of transactions and transfers, which are listed in Annex A and which are subject to any degree of liberalization.

Article 10: Exceptions to the Principle of Non-Discrimination

Special Customs or Monetary Systems

Members forming part of a special customs or monetary system may apply to one another, in addition to measures of liberalization taken in accordance with the provisions of Article 2(a), other measures of liberalization without extending them to other Members. Members forming part of such a system shall inform the Organization of its membership and those of its provisions which have a bearing on this Code.

Part II   Procedure

Article 11: Notification and Information from Members

(a) Members shall notify the Organization, within the periods which the latter may determine, of the measures of liberalization which they have taken and of any other measures which have a bearing on this Code, as well as of any modifications of such measures.

(b) Members shall notify the Organization forthwith of any cases in which they have by virtue of remark (ii) against Section I of List A of Annex A to this Code imposed restrictions on specific transactions or transfers relating to direct investments and shall state their reasons for doing so.

(c) Members shall submit to the Organization, at intervals determined by the Organization, but of no more than eighteen months, information concerning:

(i) any channels, other than official channels, through which transfers are made, and any rates of exchange applying to such transfers, if they are different from the official rates of exchange:

(ii) any security money markets and any premiums or discounts in relation to official rates of exchange prevailing therein.

(d) The Organization shall consider the notification submitted to it in accordance with the provisions of paragraphs (a), (b) and (c) with a view to determining whether each Member is complying with its obligations under this Code.

Article 12: Notification and Examination of Reservations Lodged Under Article 2(b)

(a) Each Member lodging a reservation in respect of an item

specified in List B of Annex A to the Code shall forthwith
notify the Organization of its reasons therefor.

(b) Each Member shall notify the Organization within a
period to be determined by the Organization, whether it
desires to maintain any reservation lodged by it in respect of
an item specified in List A or List B of Annex A to this Code,
and if so, state its reasons therefor.

(c) The Organization shall examine each reservation lodged
by a member in respect of an item specified in:

(i) List A at intervals of not more than eighteen
months:

(ii) List B within six months of notification, and at
intervals of not more than eighteen months thereafter;
unless the Council decides otherwise.

(d) The examinations provided for in paragraph (c) shall be
directed to making suitable proposals designed to assist
Members to withdraw their reservations.

Article 13: Notification and Examination made under Article 7

(a) Any Member invoking the provisions of Article 7 shall
notify the Organization forthwith of its action, together with
its reasons therefor.

(b) The Organization shall consider the notifications and
reasons submitted to it in accordance with the provisions of
paragraph (a) with a view to determining "whether the
Member concerned is justified in invoking the provisions of
Article 7 and, in particular, whether it is complying with the
provisions of paragraph (c) of that Article".

(c) If the action taken by a Member in accordance with the
provisions of Article 7 is not disapproved by the Organization, that action shall be reconsidered by the Organization
every six months or, subject to the provisions of Article 15
on any other date which the latter may deem appropriate.

(d) If, however, in the opinion of a Member other than the
one which has invoked Article 7, the circumstances justifying
the action taken by the latter in accordance with the
provisions of that Article have changed, that other Member
may at any time refer to the Organization for reconsideration
of the case at issue.

(e) If the action taken by a Member in accordance with the provisions of paragraph (a), (b) or (c) of Article 7 has not been disapproved by the Organization, then, if that Member subsequently invokes paragraph (a), (b) or (c) or Article 7 of the Code of Liberalization of Current Invisible Operations, or, having invoked one paragraph of Article 7 of this Code, invokes another paragraph of that Article, its case shall be reconsidered by the Organization after six months have elapsed since the date of the previous consideration, or on any other date which the latter may deem appropriate. If another Member claims that the Member in question is failing to carry out its obligations under paragraph (e) of Article 7 of this Code or paragraph (c) of Article 7 of the Code of Liberalization of Current Invisible Operations, the Organization shall consider the case without delay.

(i) If the Organization, following its consideration in accordance with paragraph (b), determines that a Member is not justified in invoking the provisions of Article 7 or is not complying with the provisions of that Article, it shall remain in consultation with the Member concerned, with a view to restoring compliance with the Code.

(ii) If, after a reasonable period of time, that Member continues to invoke the provisions of Article 7, the Organization shall reconsider the matter. If the Organization is then unable to determine that the Member concerned is justified in invoking the provisions of Article 7 or is complying with the provisions of that Article, the situation of that Member shall be examined by a special Ministerial Group, unless the Organization decides on some other exceptional procedure.

Article 14: Examination of Derogations made in accordance with Article 7 Members in Process of Economic Development

(a) In examining the case of any Member which it considers to be in the process of economic development and which has invoked the provisions of Article 7 the Organization shall have special regard to the effect that the economic development of the Member has upon its ability to carry out its obligations under paragraph (a) of Articles 1 and 2.

(b) In order to reconcile the obligations of the Member concerned under paragraph (a) of Article 2 with the requirements of its economic development, the Organization may grant that Member a special dispensation from those obligations.

Article 15: Special Report and Examination Concerning Derogations made under Article 7

(a) A Member invoking the provisions of paragraph (c) of Article 7 shall report to the Organization, within ten months after such invocation, on the measures of liberalization it has restored or proposes to restore in order to attain the objective determined in subparagraph (d) (i) of Article 7. The Member shall, if it continues to invoke these provisions, report to the Organization again on the same subject − but with reference to the objective determined in subparagraph (d) (ii) of Article 7 − within sixteen months after such invocation.

(b) If the Member considers that it will not be able to attain the objective, it shall indicate its reasons in its report and, in addition, shall state:

(i) what internal measures it has taken to restore its economic equilibrium and what results have already been attained, and

(ii) What further internal measures it proposes to take and what additional period it considers it will need in order to attain the objective determined in subparagraph (d) (i) or (d) (ii) of Article 7.

(c) In cases referred to in paragraph (b), the Organization shall consider within a period of twelve months and, if required, of eighteen months from the date on which the Member invoked the provisions of paragraph (e) of Article 7, whether the situation of that Member appears to justify its failure to attain the objective determined in sub-paragraph (d) (i) or (d) (ii) or Article 7 and whether the measures taken or envisaged and the period considered by it as necessary for attaining the objective determined, appear acceptable in the light of the objectives of the Organization in the commercial and financial fields.

(d) If a Member invokes the provisions of both paragraph (c) of Article 7 of this Code and paragraph (c) of Article 7 of the Code of Liberalization of Current Invisible Operations the periods of twelve and eighteen months referred to in paragraph (c) shall run from the date of the earlier invocation.

(e) If following any of the examinations provided for in paragraph (c) the Organization is unable to approve the arguments advanced by the Member concerned in accordance with the provisions of paragraph (b) the situation of that Member shall be examined by a special Ministerial Group, unless the Organization decides on some other exceptional procedure.

Article 16: Reference to the Organization Internal Arrangements

(Not reproduced)

Article 17: Reference to the Organization Retention, Introduction or Reintroduction of Restrictions

(Not reproduced)

Part III   Terms of Reference

Article 18: Committee for Invisible Transactions General Tasks

(a) The Committee for Invisible Transactions shall consider all questions concerning the interpretation or implementation of the provisions of this Code or other Acts of the Council relating to the liberalization of capital movements and the use of non-resident owned funds and shall report its conclusions thereon to the Council as appropriate.

(b) The Committee for Invisible Transactions shall submit to the Council any appropriate proposals in connection with its tasks as defined in paragraph (a) and, in particular, with the extension of measures of liberalization as provided in Article 1 of this Code.

Article 19:

(This article refers to a number of matters which are mainly of a procedural character and is not reproduced here.)

Article 20:

(Not reproduced)

Part IV   Miscellaneous

(Not reproduced)

Selected Bibliography

Set out below is a selected bibliography of works, mainly in English, on some of the principal activities in the service sector, focusing in particular on international transactions. Having been prepared for general as well as specialist readers, it has been confined to books; journal articles have been put to one side. From the vast literature on the development of the world economy, a selection has been made, in the first section of the bibliography, of contributions relating to recent issues. In the next two sections are listed a number of studies on non-tariff barriers to *visible* trade and restrictive business practices. The remaining sections deal with banking, insurance, shipping and tourism.

ISSUES RELATING TO THE WORLD TRADING SYSTEM

HENRY G. AUBREY, *Atlantic Economic Cooperation: the Case of the OECD* (New York: Praeger, for the Council on Foreign Relations, 1967).

C. FRED BERGSTEN *et al.*, *Reshaping the International Economic Order* (Washington: Brookings Institution, 1972).

THOMAS BLAND *et al.*, *Britain's Invisible Earnings*, Report of the Committee on Invisible Exports (London: British National Export Council, 1967).

SIR ALEC CAIRNCROSS *et al.*, *Economic Policy for the European Community: the Way Forward* (London: Macmillan, for the Institut für Weltwirtschaft an der Universität Kiel, 1974).

W. M. CLARKE, *The City in the World Economy* (London: Institute of Economic Affairs, 1965).

RICHARD N. COOPER, *The Economics of Interdependence* (New York: McGraw-Hill, for the Council on Foreign Relations, 1963).

HUGH CORBET and ROBERT JACKSON (eds), *In Search of a New World Economic Order* (London: Croom Helm, for the Trade Policy Research Centre, 1974).

W. M. CORDEN, *Trade Policy and Economic Welfare* (Oxford: Clarendon Press, 1974).

GERARD CURZON, *Multilateral Commercial Diplomacy* (London: Michael Joseph, 1965).

KENNETH W. DAM, *The GATT Law and International Economic Organization* (Chicago and London: University of Chicago Press, 1970).

WILLIAM DIEBOLD, Jr, *The United States and the Industrial World: American Foreign Economic Policy in the 1970s* (New York: Praeger, for the Council on Foreign Relations, 1972).

ROBERT HAWKINS and INGO WALTER (eds), *The United States and International Trade: Commercial Policy Options in an Age of Controls* (Lexington: D.C. Heath, 1972).

HIGH-LEVEL GROUP ON TRADE AND RELATED PROBLEMS, *Policy Perspectives for International Trade and Economic Relations,* Rey Report (Paris: OECD Secretariat, 1972).

HELEN HUGHES (ed.), *Prospects for Partnership: Industrial and Trade Policies in the 1970s* (Baltimore: Johns Hopkins University Press, for the International Bank for Reconstruction and Development, 1973).

HARRY G. JOHNSON, *Comparative Costs and Commercial Policy Theory for a Developing World Economy* (Stockholm: Almqvist and Wicksell, 1968).

CHARLES P. KINDELBERGER and ANDREW SCHONFIELD (eds), *North American and Western European Economic Policies* (London: Macmillan, for the International Economic Association, 1971).

KAREN KOCK, *International Trade Policy and the GATT 1947-67* (Stockholm: Almqvist and Wicksell, 1969).

FRANK McFADZEAN *et al.*, *Towards an Open World Economy,* Report of an Advisory Group (London: Macmillan, for the Trade Policy Research Centre, 1972).

GARDNER PATTERSON, *Discrimination in International Trade: Policy Issues 1945-65* (Princeton: Princeton University Press, 1966).

ERNEST H. PREEG, *Traders and Diplomats* (Washington: Brookings Institution, 1970).

PRESIDENTIAL COMMISSION ON INTERNATIONAL TRADE AND INVESTMENT POLICY, *United States International Economic Policy in an Interdependent World,* Williams Report (Washington: US Government Printing Office, 1971), with two volumes of technical papers under the same title.

DAVID ROBERTSON, *International Trade Policy* (London: Macmillan, 1972).

PAUL A. SAMUELSON (ed.), *International Economic Relations* (London: Macmillan, for the International Economic Association, 1969).

The United States and the European Community: Policies for a Changing World (New York: Committee for Economic Development, 1971).

US Foreign Economic Policy for the 1970s: a New Approach to New Realities, a Policy Report by a NPA Advisory Committee (Washington: National Planning Association, 1971).

World Invisible Trade (London: Committee on Invisible Exports), annual publication.

INVISIBLE BARRIERS TO *VISIBLE* TRADE

ROBERT E. BALDWIN, *Non-tariff Distortions of International Trade* (Washington: Brookings Institution, 1970).

GERARD and VICTORIA CURZON, *Hidden Barriers to International Trade,* Thames Essay No. 1 (London: Trade Policy Research Centre, 1970).

GERARD and VICTORIA CURZON, *Global Assault on Non-tariff Trade Barriers,* Thames Essay No. 3 (London: Trade Policy Research Centre, 1972).

GEOFFREY DENTON and SEAMUS O'CLEIREACAIN, *Subsidy Issues in International Commerce,* Thames Essay No. 5 (London: Trade Policy Research Centre, 1972).

GEOFFREY DENTON, SEAMUS O'CLEIREACAIN and SALLY ASH, *Trade Effects of Public Subsidies to Private Enterprise* (London: Macmillan, for the Trade Policy Research Centre, 1975).

BRIAN HINDLEY, *Britain's Position on Non-tariff Protection,* Thames Essay No. 4 (London: Trade Policy Research Centre, 1972).

PETER LLOYD, *Non-tariff Distortions of Australian Trade* (Canberra: Australian National University Press, 1973).

HARALD B. MALMGREN, *Trade Wars or Trade Negotiations: Non-tariff Barriers and Economic Peace-keeping* (Washington: Atlantic Council of the United States, 1970).

ROBERT MIDDLETON, *Negotiating on Non-tariff Distortions of Trade: the EFTA Precedents* (London: Macmillan, for the Trade Policy Research Centre, 1975).

CAROLINE PESTIEAU and JACQUES HENRY, *Non-tariff Trade Barriers as a Problem in International Development* (Montreal: C. D. Howe Research Institute, 1972).

KLAUS STEGEMANN, *Canadian Non-tariff Distortions of International Trade* (Montreal: C. D. Howe Research Institute, 1973).

RESTRICTIVE BUSINESS PRACTICES

Restrictive Business Practices: Article 15 of the Convention, Report of the Working Party, EFTA Document 63/65 (Geneva: EFTA Secretariat, 1965).

Restrictive Business Practices: Article 15 of the Convention, Report of the Second Working Party, EFTA Document 41/68 (Geneva: EFTA Secretariat, 1968).

Restrictive Business Practices (Geneva: GATT Secretariat, 1959).

Market Power and the Law (Paris: OECD Secretariat, 1970).

Comparative Summary of Legislations on Restrictive Business Practices, mimeographed (Paris: OECD Secretariat, 1971).

Restrictive Business Practices, Report by the UNCTAD Secretariat, mimeographed, UNCTAD Document TD/122/Supplement (Geneva: UNCTAD, 1972).

Restrictive Business Practices, Studies on the United Kingdom of Great Britain and Northern Ireland, the United States of America and Japan (New York: United Nations, 1973).

MARK S. MASSEL, *Competition and Monopoly: Legal and Economic Issues* (Washington: Brookings Institution, 1963).

ADRIENNE SZOKOLOCZY-SYLLABA, *The Interpretation of the Frustration Clause in Article 15 of the Stockholm Convention,* Annex 1 EFTA Document INF 16/68 (Geneva: EFTA Secretariat, 1968).

ADRIENNE SZOKOLOCAY-SYLLABA, *EFTA: Restrictive Business Practices* (Bern: Stampfli, 1973).

BANKING

DAVID A. ALHADEFF, *Competition and Controls in Banking: a Study of the Regulation of Bank Competition in Italy, France and England* (Berkeley: University of California Press, 1968).

Banking in a Changing World, Lectures and Proceedings at the 24th International Banking Summer School (Rome: Associazone Bancaria Italiana, 1971).

WILLIAM J. BROWN, *The Dual Banking System in the United States* (New York: American Bankers Association, 1968).

The Business of Banking, Papers and Discussions at the 26th International Banking Summer School (London: Institute of Bankers, 1973).

Capital Markets in Atlantic Economic Relationships (Paris: Atlantic Institute, 1967).

Development of Capital Markets (London: International Federation of Stock Exchanges,1969).

The Development of a European Capital Market (Brussels: EEC Commission, 1966).

PAUL EINZIG, *The Case Against Nationalization of the Banks* (London: Macmillan, 1973).

GERALD C. FISCHER, *American Banking Structure* (New York: Columbia University Press, 1968).

BRIAN GRIFFITHS, *Competition in Banking* (London: Institute of Economic Affairs, 1971).

PETER C. LUNN and BERNARD S. WHEBLE, *British Banks and International Trade,* Ernest Sykes Memorial Lectures (London: Institute of Bankers, 1972).

E. B. NORTHCLIFFE, *Taxes on the Issue and Negotiation of Securities* (Paris: OECD Secretariat, 1970).

STUART W. ROBINSON, *Multinational Banking: a Study of Certain Legal and Financial Aspects of the Postwar Operations of the United States Branch Banks in Western Europe* (Leiden: A. W. Sijthoff, 1972).

FRANK RAYMOND RYDER, *Legal Problems of Foreign Banking: An Examination with Some Solutions of the Difficulties Facing British Bankers Involved in Foreign Transactions* (London: Waterlow, 1971).
ALAN A. WALTERS (ed.), *Money and Banking* (Harmondsworth: Penguin, 1973).

INSURANCE

R. L. CARTER, *The Economics of Insurance* (London: Policy Holder Press, 1973).
R. L. CARTER (ed.), *Handbook of Insurance* (London: Kluwer-Harrap Handbooks, 1973).
R. L. CARTER and NEIL DOHERTY (eds), *Handbook of Risk Management* (London: Kluwer-Harrap Handbooks, 1974).
Financial Guarantees Required from Life Assurance Concerns, OECD Insurance Committee (Paris: OECD Secretariat, 1971).
JAMES GOLLIN, *Pay Now, Die Later: a Report on Life Insurance, America's Biggest and Strangest Industry* (Harmondsworth: Penguin Books, 1968).
M. GROSSMAN *et al., Insurance Markets of the World* (Zurich: Swiss Reinsurance Corporation, 1964).
JAN HELLNER and GUNNAR NORD, *Life Insurance Law in International Perspective,* Reports on an International Colloquium held in 1967 (Lund: Berlingska Boktryckeriet, 1969).
The Insurance Industry in Britain (London: Central Office of Information, 1968).
LAWRENCE D. JONES, *Investment Policies of Life Insurance Companies* (Boston: Harvard University Graduate School of Business Administration, 1968).
Report of the Seventh Conference of European Insurance Supervisory Services (Berlin: Bundesaufsichstant für das Versicherungs und Bausparwesen, 1970).
Supervision of Private Insurance in Europe, OECD Document 15/283 (Paris: OECD Secretariat, 1963).

SHIPPING

ESRA BENNATHAN and ALAN A. WALTERS, *The Economics of Ocean Freight Rates* (New York: Praeger, 1969).
BRIAN MEASURES DEAKIN, in collaboration with T. SEWARD, *Shipping Conferences: a Study of their Origin, Development and Economic Practices,* Occasional Paper No. 37 (Cambridge: Cambridge University Press, for the Cambridge Department of Applied Economics, 1973).
The Jones Act (Washington: United States Transportation Institute, 1966).

OLAV KNUDSEN, *The Politics of International Shipping: Conflict and Interaction in a Transnational Issue Area 1946-68* (Lexington: D. C. Heath, 1973).

SAMUEL A. LAWRENCE, *International Sea Transport: the Years Ahead* (Lexington: D. C. Heath, 1972).

Non-tariff Obstacles to Trade (Paris: International Chamber of Commerce, 1969), Annex V, "Flag Discrimination".

Report of the Committee of Enquiry into Shipping, Rochdale Report, Cmnd. 4337 (London: HM Stationery Office, 1970).

Short-sea Shipping: the Report of the Economic Development Committee for the Movement of Exports (London: National Economic Development Office, 1970).

S. G. STURMEY, *British Shipping and World Competition* (London: Athlone Press, 1962).

Subsidies: a Summary of the Principal Subsidies and Aids Granted by the Major Foreign Maritime Nations to their Shipping and Shipbuilding Industries (Washington: United States Maritime Administration, 1962).

TOURISM

Economic Review of World Tourism (Geneva: International Union of Official Travel Organizations [IUOTO]), biennial publication.

International Tourism and Tourism Policy in OECD Member Countries (Paris: OECD Secretariat, 1971).

International Travel Statistics (Geneva: IUOTO), annual publication.

D. McEWEN, *The European Tourist Markets* (London: Tourism Planning and Research, 1971).

M. PETERS, *International Tourism* (London: Hutchinson, 1969).

Index

Agriculture, "special position", 32
Air transport, 5, 20, 31, 33, 37, 105
Anti-dumping Code, 96

Balance of payments, 1, 2, 5, 14, 15, 20, 31, 36, 63, 64, 83, 84, 85, 90, 92, 107
Balanced growth, need for, 79
Bank Act, 74, 75
Banking, 5, 33-5, 41, 56-7, 73-5, 90, 92, 98
  bibliography, 172
  developing countries, 117-22
  OECD countries, 114-17
  reserve requirements, 43-4
'Barrier-by-barrier' approach, 93, 94
Bilateral agreements, 92
Borrowing and lending, 42-3, 63
Brokerage, 6

Cabotage laws, 59, 72
Capital markets, world, 21-9
Capital movement, 33-4, 39, 61-4, 79-81, 108, 159
  general code on, 97, 109-10
Cargo Preference Act, 38
CENSA, 99
Civil aviation, see Air transport
Code of Conduct, 95-6
Code of Liberalization of Capital Movements, 85, 88, 89, 155-8
Code of Liberalization of Current Invisible Operations, 85, 86, 88, 89, 104, 159-68

Code of Liberalization of Invisible Transactions, 84
Compensation, 49
Competition, 32, 35-7, 39-40, 48
Compulsory cessions, 53-4, 140-2
Conference lines, 77
Constraints of other countries, retaliation against, 75-9
Credit restraint, 43
Currency restrictions, 60

Direct investment, 6, 33-4, 39, 61, 67
  developing countries, 126-33
  OECD countries, 122-6
Domestic ownership of key industries, 72
Domestication, insurance, 49-50, 135

Economic policy, 70, 74
Economic research, 68-9
EEC, 32, 46-7
EFTA, 32
Employment of expatriates, 55, 143-4
Euro-bonds, 21
Euro-currencies, 21
Euro-currency markets, 21, 24, 28, 80
Euro-dollar market, 21, 28
European Payments Union, 84
Exchange control, 38-9, 44, 51-2, 83, 96
Exchange rate, 67, 68
Expatriates, employment of, 55, 143-4

Exports and imports, commission on, 6

Factor-input mix, constraints on choice of, 41
Films, 6
Financial services, 35, 98
Fiscal measures, 43
Flag discrimination, 57-9, 72, 76, 79
Foreign bond issues, 29
Foreign competition, *see* Competition
Foreign currency, 80
Foreign Direct Investment Programme, 90
Foreign exchange, *see* Exchange control
Foreign securities, 63
Free trade, 83
Funds, localization of, 52

GATT, 3, 11, 83, 93, 96, 103, 109
GNP, 14, 15, 86
Government discrimination, insurance, 53-5
Government procurement, 37-8, 78
Government services and transfers, 4
Gross national product, 7, 14, 15, 86

High-level Group on Trade and Related Problems, 104

IATA, 32, 33
IMF, 3, 80
Imports and exports, commission on, 6
Infant-industry argument, 70-2
Insurance, 5, 33, 37, 45-56, 73, 104, 133-44
  bibliography, 173
  compulsory cessions, 53-4, 140-2

domestication, 49-50, 135
employment of expatriates, 55, 143-4
government discrimination, 53-5
localization of funds, 52, 138-40
nationalization, 48
prohibitions abroad, 50-1, 136
public procurement, 54-5, 143
restriction of foreign competition, 48
restrictions on remittances, 137
UNCTAD, 56
Interest, dividends, profits and royalties, 6, 106
Interest equalization tax, 43, 63, 90
Interest payments on deposits, control of, 42
Interest rate differentials, 80
Inter-firm agreements, 32
International bond market, 21, 29
International monetary system, *see* IMF
International transactions, 8-9
Investments
  direct, *see* Direct investment
  earnings from, 106
  portfolio, *see* Portfolio investments
Invisible trade
  analysis of barriers, 31-66
  balances of, 11
  British, 14-21
  comparison with visible, 2
  components of, 4-7
  constraints on earnings from, 1
  defence of barriers to, 67-82
  general code, 97, 109-10
  illustrative list of discriminatory constraints, 113-54
  liberalization of, 84-7
  measures of dependence on, 12-14
  nature and importance of, 1-30
  top ten invisible earning countries, 14

total value, 11
types of constraints, 34-5
use of term, 1-2
world, 7-29

Johnson, Harry G., 68, 71, 110
Jones Act, 72

Labour, 41
Lending and borrowing, 42-3, 63
Liberalization List, 61
Liberalization of invisible trade, 84-7
Liner conference, 78
Lloyd Brasiliero, 76
Lloyd's underwriters, 45, 46
Localization of funds, 52, 138-40

McFadzean Report, 106
Malinowski, W. R., 73
Maritime freights, 88
Marshall aid, 84
Mercantile Bank, 74
Merchanting, 6
Monetary policy, 74
Most-favoured-nation (MFN) principle, 93-5
Movement of capital, *see* Capital movements
Multilateral negotiations, 93-5

Nationalization, insurance, 48
Non-discrimination, principle of, 95
Non-tariff barriers, 83, 93, 94
use of term, 1
Non-tariff distortions, 1
Non-tariff interventions, 1

OECD, 32, 47, 83, 85-91, 103, 105, 106, 109; *see also* Code for Liberalization of Capital Movements, Code for Liberalization of Current Invisible Operations
OEEC, 83, 84
Oil, price of, 9
Oil-producing countries, 9

Policy research, 69
Portfolio investments, 7, 34, 41-2, 62-4, 67, 102
Private sector, 20
relative stability, of type of invisible earnings, 20
Private transfers, 7
Product mix, constraints on choice of, 40
Protection policies, 35-6
Public assistance, 78
Public procurement, 54-5, 143
Public sector, 20

Reciprocity, principle of, 95
Reinsurance, 45, 47
UNCTAD, 56
Remittance, restrictions on, 52
Reserve requirements, 43-4
Restrictive business practices, 32
bibliography, 171-2
Retaliation, 91
Rey Report, 104, 106
Rochdale Report, 59
Royalties, 6

Services, 45
classification of, 31
flow of currently-produced, 31-3
growth of, 7-8
importance of, 8
Shipbuilding, 32-3
Shipping, 4, 31, 33, 37, 40, 57-60, 70, 76-8, 98
bibliography, 173
cabotage laws, 59
developing countries, 146-53
flag discrimination, 57-9, 72, 76, 79
OECD countries, 144-6
subsidies, 59-60
see also Transport
Stock exchanges, 63
Sturmey, S. G., 76
Subsidies, shipping, 59-60
Sylvester, Vice Admiral John, 72

Tariffs, 93
Taxation, 43, 63, 90
Television, 6
Tokyo Round, 11, 103, 104
Tourism, *see* Travel
Trade Act of 1974, 103
Transport, 4, 31, 35, 40, 98; *see also* Air transport, Shipping
Travel, 5, 39, 60-1, 106
 bibliography, 174
 currency restrictions, 60
 developing countries, 154
 OECD countries, 153

UNCTAD, 56, 59, 70, 73, 76, 83, 99

Unilateral action, 96
United Kingdom, 11, 14-21
 external liabilities and claims of banks in non-sterling currencies, 22
United States, 11

Visible trade
 comparison with invisible, 2
 invisible barriers to, bibliography, 171
Voluntary Foreign Credit Restraint Programme, 90

World trading system, bibliography, 169-70

DATE DUE

JAN 15 '88

JAN 04 '91

DEMCO 38-297